Narcissist

How to Handle a Narcissist and Heal from Hidden Emotional and Psychological Abuse and what you need to Understand to Deal with a Range of Narcissistic Personalities

SIMONDYER MILLER

Table of Contents

Introduction

Random acts of violence, manipulation, and assault occur on a day-to-day basis all over the world. People can be injured and violated by complete strangers. But what is it like when the person you trust the most, perhaps a partner, a parent, a sibling, an authority figure, is the sole individual responsible for the most mental and emotional pain a human can endure?

This is when the conscious decision to cause harm on a consistent basis to another human falls into the classification of abuse. [1]According to The National Domestic Violence Hotline, 24 people per minute on average are victims of rape, physical violence or stalking by a close partner in the US. Domestic violence within a household is also 40% more likely to include child abuse within the home as well.

But what happens when abuse is more hidden? What happens when it does not show its face through a bruise, aberrant behavior, missing days of work, or hospital visits?

Emotional abuse and its link to narcissistic personality traits in perpetratore that act as parents, partners and authority figures is what will be discussed in this book. This book will also explore

---

[1] https://www.thehotline.org/resources/statistics/

and encourage the bravery necessary in order to escape a partner or an emotionally damaging past that is effecting your present contentment. It is chiefly essential to recognize this as early on in the process of recovery as possible: no form of abuse, is anyone's fault.

In this book, there will be a serious of quotes spoken by people who are victims of narcissistic emotional/psychological abuse. These quotes are directly taken from a collection called *Narcissism: A Book of Quotes: A selection of quotes from the collective wisdom of over 12,000 individual discussions*. They were collected together from a discussion board, where victims voiced their experiences of abuse with narcissist personalities. The site heard from victims over 18 months on the website *Suite 101: Narcissistic Personality Disorder Discussion Site*. These will be references to help the individuals reading this book that they are not alone in their experience of emotional/psychological abuse.

Chapter 1: The Basics of Psychological Abuse

"It is excruciating pain. It is the pain of separation, the pain of loss, the pain of dreams and expectations unrealized. It is the loss and death of a mirage."

Abuse is defined by behaviors committed in order to intentionally cause harm. There are many kinds of abuse that can be committed
 by both men and women to either the same or opposing gender and identified sexuality. The different forms of abuse can be divided into two separate categories, with similar and associated umbrella terms. The three categories of abuse are the behaviors that fall under domestic abuse/violence, child abuse, and elder abuse.

Domestic Abuse: Occurs when a partner physically, verbally, emotionally, sexually and technologically causes harm to their significant other. The definitions of these behaviors can occur independently or blend into multiple forms of abuse in a relationship.

Physical: Striking, punching, slapping, being held down, throwing items at partner.

According to the New York State Office of Children and Family Services, physical abuse is defined as [2]"non-accidental use of force that results in bodily injury." Those who are physically abused are not limited by age. Children as well as adults can be victims of physical abuse. The most common physical abuse though are women, vulnerable elderly, those with mental health issues, those who are physically disabled, substance users, those with developmental delays, and intimate partners.

Physical abuse often occurs in conjunction with emotional, verbal, and sometimes sexual abuse. The general cycle of abuse usually occurs as follows:

1. Threats of Violence: Threatening violence against a partner, child, sibling, either specific to the action or a general statement to cause immense fear. For example, a partner may accidentally spill milk onto their partner's pants, and the abuser threatens that they "will pay for that later."

2. Physical Abuse Itself: The act that was threatened is followed through upon. This can occur in the presence of children, one-on-one, or with the child itself. Examples of this physical abuse can

---

[2] https://www.healthyplace.com/abuse/adult-physical-abuse/what-is-physical-abuse

range from choking, to slapping, to kicking, to locking a child or partner inside another room or cupboard.

3. Apologies by the Abuser: The abuser appears to feel guilty and immensely sorry for the pain they inflicted upon their partner, child, or sibling. The abuser is generally extra attentive, kinder, more generous, and even buys gifts or plans special trips for the personal that they abused.

4. The Cycle Repeats: The threats of violence begin again once the abuser feels they have apologized enough with their behavior. Often, guilt and shame are evoked, as the abuser accuses their victim as being the one to 'trigger' their unacceptable behavior.

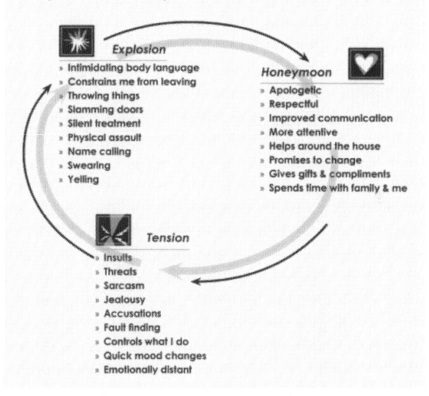

The following graphic can be seen as a general summarization of the cycle of abuse as a whole. In this version, all forms of abuse are isolated into three separate sections titled: *Honeymoon, Tension,* and *Explosion.* These stages condense the varying behaviors of domestic abusers and illustrate the endless reality of the abuse.

Verbal: Name-calling, false accusations.

This form of abuse generally falls under the same category as emotional/psychological abuse, as it generally occurs at the same time. Verbal abuse can be utilized through the use of actual words, or that or body language that implies the intended put down.

Although verbal abuse is often defined as simply the use of name-calling, a vast array of behaviors has been observed by psychologists that don't all appear to be too obvious. Patricia Evans notes a couple of examples in her book [3]*The Verbally Abusive Relationship:*

1. Withholding: When a person intentionally withholds information that is necessary in order to maintain a growing and healthy relationship. This can occur in both romantic and parental relationships alike. The person holds back their thoughts and feelings, merely delivering information that is factual. The goal here is to avoid engagement with their partner or important individual in their life.

2. Countering: When an individual is intentionally argumentative, discounting another person's feelings and thoughts on a regular basis. The abuser often times attempts to convince the other person that their feelings are wrong. An

[3] https://www.psychologytoday.com/ca/blog/the-mysteries-love/201503/15-common-forms-verbal-abuse-in-relationships

example of this is when a person's shares their interest in a certain type of music, and their partner denies that their feelings toward the genre are actually valid.

3. Discounting: This kind of behavior is a form of criticism. The abuser denies the victim's perspective as invalid, completely wrong. The abuser may make statements like the other individual is 'too sensitive,' or, 'makes a big deal out of everything.' The victim's feelings are constantly denied and not seen as anything the abuser wants to acknowledge as being relevant.

4. Disguised as jokes: The abuser may make a statement that is hurtful, and simply reacts as if the behavior was a joke, once again invaliding the victim on their natural reactions and feelings.

5. Blocking and diverting: This is a form of withholding, where the abuser makes great effort to control various topics of conversation. The abuser may accuse their victim of having too much of an opinion, or talking 'out of turn'.

6. Denial: This can become abusive when it is consisting and always puts a halt to a relationship. The abuser always tries to justify or rationalize their behavior, never being able to admit that they had done anything wrong. This once again invalidates the victim's feelings.

7. Abusive Anger: Yelling, screaming, name-calling a child, partner or parent is a common form of verbal abuse.

8. Forgetting: This falls under the category of abuse when it occurs on a consistent basis. If the abuser actually did forget an important date or event, they would still be unable to admit their mistake due to denial.

9. Ordering: Telling someone what to do on a consistent basis in an angry and expectant manner is abuse, no matter who is doing the speaking. This is where the concept of control comes into play for abusers.

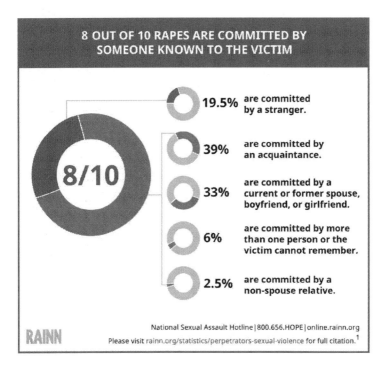

Sexual: Forcing partner to have sexual intercourse or participate in sexual activities.

Sexual abuse can occur between various age groups, races, genders, and sexualities. In this section, sexual abuse that is perpetrated upon adults will be discussed.

Sexual violence is a term that covers a multitude of actions that occur in a non-consensual interaction. The various forms defined here can occur between strangers, intimate partners, neighbors, family members, and can either occur in one single instance or an over years of consistent abuse. The definitions are divided into categories, which are sexual assault and sexual harassment. All actions fall under the category of being done without consent.

Sexual Assault

-Rape: When sexual intercourse is initiated without both sides consent. This could include the insertion of a bodily organ into another, or the insertion of an object. Rape does occur between married and devoted spouses. In a study conducted in 2014 by [4]Tario and Associates, it was found that thirty percent of all adult rape case were committed by partners. In the same study it was reported that of the women that reported being raped by their marital partner, 69% reported that occurring more than once.

-Assault: Behavior of a sexual nature that is unwanted by the victim. These behaviors could include various forms of groping,

---

[4] https://www.tariolaw.com/shocking-marital-rape-statistics/

attempted rape, touching of genitals, forcing oral sex, and using objects in a sexual manner. Sexual assault occurs in relationships, and effects the victim just as much as assaults that are committed by strangers or acquaintance Interfering.

Sexual Harassment

-**Extortion:** Using blackmail in order to force a person to engage in sexual and unwanted acts.

-**Indecent Act:** An act performed by an abuser in order to cause embarrassment or humiliation. Forms of indecent acts are flashing, self-masturbation, cat-calling, honking car horns, and yelling obscenities.

-**Propositions:** Continuously proposal dates, outings, or get-togethers with an individual who has repeatedly denied advances. This kind of sexual harassment includes sexual descriptions or attempts at flirtation that are graphic and inappropriate in nature.

-**Remarks:** Commenting on an individual's appearance in a sexual manner that is unwanted by the subject of the remarks.

-**Posting Photos:** This is also a form of technological abuse, that can occur between co-workers, schoolmates, and romantic partners. This happens when an abuser posts a photo or video that is meant to degrade another person's sexuality or to continue unwanted advances toward this person.

-Exploitation: Repeated sexual advances committed in order to exploit them due to feelings of rejection.

Technological: Stalking and tracking their partner without permission.

Technological abuse is a form of abuse that is becoming more and more recognized as our presence on social media continues to increase. Many people who are in domestically abusive situations have recognized cellphones and the internet as yet another tool their partner utilizes to continue controlling and abusing them. [5]The Women's Media Center highlighted the four main ways in which abusers attempt to control their victims:

1. Interfering in the victim's use of technology. This could include locking the person out of their social media accounts, or limiting their use on them.
2. Pretending to be the survivor on various accounts in order to harass the family and friends of the victim.
3. Sending messages through various forms of messaging devices such as text and email.
4. Tracking the victim with spying software within technological devices such as cellphones, laptops, or using hidden cameras.

---

[5] http://www.womensmediacenter.com/speech-project/technology-abuse-its-still-about-power-control

Even through the application of privacy settings, dedicated abusers will apply a variety of methods in order to continue abusing their victim. Parents will go through their child's account, create fake accounts, or use a friend's account in order to stalk them virtually.

Emotional/Psychological: Intentionally causing shame or guilt, manipulating, playing mind games.

This is the specific form of abuse that will be focused on in this book. Although emotional abuse does occur often between siblings and parents of children, this section will focus on emotional/psychological abuse that occurs between adults.

The general intention of emotional/psychological abuse is control and degradation.

Emotional/psychological abuse without physical or sexual abuse is the most hidden form of mistreatment between two or more people. Because this behavior primarily occurs verbally, many people are unaware that they are victims of abuse until a loved one points it out. The vulnerability of the victim of emotional/psychological abuse is highly connected to that of a narcissistic abuser, but that will be covered later in this book.

Examples of emotional/psychological abuse are as follows:

-Criticisms of physical appearance.

-Criticism of intelligence.

-Name-calling intended to bring down the victim's self-esteem

-Character assassination involved a label of a person's behavior: for example, if you are late for one event, you are 'always' late. This is an attempt to make someone feel like a bad person.

-Public embarrassment occurs when an abuser insults someone in public.

-Abusers can greatly put down their partner or other individual's interests. This is meant to remove a victim from a situation that their partner is not involved in.

-Making threats against the children or those the victim cares about.

-The abuser may want to know where you are at all time, and may show up just to make sure you were where you said you were.

-Constant lecturing about any mistakes you made.

-Ordering around the victim like a child; telling them what to wear, to eat, who they can be with outside the house.

-Using jealousy to make the victim feel guilty.

-Denying that an argument or agreement took place is called gaslighting. This makes the abused question their own mental stability.

-Blaming the victim for all of their problems.

-Abusers often deny that abuse is occurring and turn the issue around to the victim, saying that they are the cause of the abuse.

Most victims of this form of abuse do not recognize these behaviors as just that because the person would 'never hit them.' People in these situations of emotional/psychological abuse feel as if they are losing their minds, have low self-esteem, feel worthless, and feel like their partner is correct in their entire negative assessment of them.

Child Abuse: Occurs when an authority, parent or sibling physically, verbally, emotionally or sexually intentionally causes harm to a minor from age 0-18. The following are examples of the most common forms of abuse that occur to children.

Neglect: The failure to provide basic needs to a child such as shelter, nourishment, adequate supervision, and proper emotional comfort.

According to data gathered by child welfare agencies in Canada, [6]34% of child abuse cases accounted for issues of neglect. People who neglect their children do not provide the right clothing, a place to live, a healthy diet, good hygiene, a safe environment to live in, exercise, fresh air, and moral guidance. Neglect can fall under the category of physical and emotional.

---

[6] https://www.canada.ca/en/public-health/services/health-promotion/stop-family-violence/problem-canada.html

A child can be a suspected victim of neglect through displaying a wide variety of symptoms. Examples of what to look out for are as follows:

Consistent Absences: The child is often absent from school or social gatherings, without much or any believable excuses.

Stealing Food: The child consistently takes food from other students or stores where they feel they cannot be caught.

Exhibits body odor: A child may be constantly dirty or emit a foul stench, or wear the same clothes every day.

Telling teacher/other Care giver: A child may be vocal enough to provide another caregiving with information that informs them that there is not a parent or supervisor available in order to provide them with care.

Emotional neglect toward a child may include the detail of affection, allowing a child to use drugs or alcohol, not getting the child the physical or emotional care they need, or allowing anti-social behavior such as assault and verbal abuse of others.

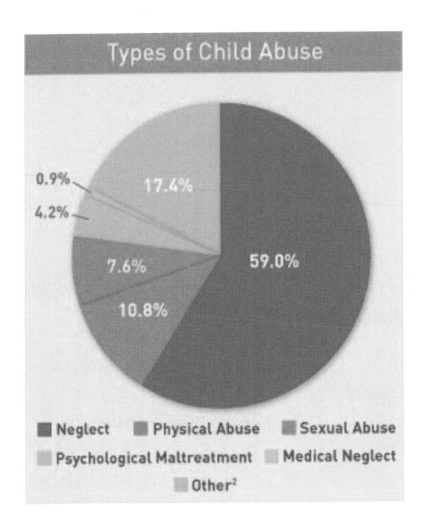

Types of Child Abuse

0.9%
4.2%
17.4%
7.6%
59.0%
10.8%

■ Neglect   ■ Physical Abuse   ■ Sexual Abuse
■ Psychological Maltreatment   ■ Medical Neglect
■ Other[2]

Physical: Striking, spanking, pulling, punching.

Physical abuse is the second most occurring form of child abuse that is reported. Physical abuse occurs when a parents or adult inflicts physical pain on a child, whether or not it was intended. The accidental cause of pain may be the result of too severe a form of discipline. A lot of parents who abuse their children believe that they are applying appropriate discipline toward their child in

18

order to help them learn. This is indeed not the case, as there is a vast difference between discipline a child and physically abusing them.

These three tactics are generally applied as a parent or guardian toward the child/children that are being abused:

-Applying Unpredictability: The child does not know what will set their abuser off. It could be spilled cereal, making a spelling mistake on a test, or not coming home on time. They are vastly unaware as to what behavior will trigger a physical attack. The child is constantly anxious and weary of their abusive parent.

-Lashing out in anger: Anger is a normal emotion, but when parents use it as a way to control their children, they are negatively associated the emotion, which will make it harder for the child to process once they grow up. The association will become concrete; the more intense the anger is coming from the parent, the more painful and abusive the results will be.

-Fear as a method to control: Constantly fearing physical abuse from a parent is a way that many parents attempt to teach their children to behave. It is a false belief that the fear of pain will shape an individual in a positive manner. They are more than like to simply fear the pain, and therefore choose to behave to avoid that occurrence. This once again always them to associate anger with violence.

Examples of physical abuse range from striking a child, spanking, burning, locking a child away in a room or cupboard, etc. Blending neglectful behavior with the physical abuse may also occur, such as not changing a child's diaper as a method of punishment for not using a toilet properly.

Verbal: Insulting, degrading, minimizing achievements, name-calling.

Verbal abuse toward child is very similar to verbal abuse that occurrences against an adult. It is very common, and more than likely the most unseen and overlooked kind of abuse that happens to child. Demoralizing or yelling constantly at a child can be confused for discipline. But in reality, these behaviors can have a livelong effect on the child. Studies over the years have shown that verbal abuse is capable of causing depression and anxiety in a young adult, to aid them in developing an inferiority complex, which in turn destroys their self esteem. Behaviors such as yelling at a child for a mistake, degrading their accomplishments, insulting their intelligence, and shaming them for their interests and opinions.

Sexual: Molestation and grooming of a child to be used for sexual purposes.

A child is unable to consent to any sexual activity, therefore, any act that is sexual in nature with a child involved connotes abuse. Childhood sexual abuse is far-reaching, and has the ability to cause some of the most severe mental health and addictions issues for the child later in life. Sexual abuse committed against a child does not always come in the form of direct skin to skin contact with the child. Direct sex, fondling, or forced masturbation are of course forms of sexual abuse, but other acts that include exposing oneself to a minor, sharing graphic images with a minor, or engaging inappropriate digital interaction with a minor fall under the category of sexual abuse.

Most perpetratore of child abuse are individuals that the child knows. According to RAINN, as many as 93% of victims of child abuse under the age of 18 know the person who abused them. This is not always a parent, but another family member, caregiver, older sibling, or person who is present and manipulative enough to use the child for their sole benefit of abusing.

There are many physical signs of sexual abuse that parents and loved ones can look out for. Some of the most common symptoms are bleeding or bruising in the genital area, stained or ripped underclothes, yeast infections, difficulty sitting or walking, and painful, itching or burning in the genital area. Behavioral signs that a child is being sexually abused depends upon the child's personality.

Emotional/Psychological: Rejecting, isolating, ignoring, guilting and shaming.

Many of the behaviors that are utilized in emotionally/psychologically abusing adults can be applied to children, but with more ease. Children are vulnerable and malleable, so it is easy to injure the self-worth of a person who is still growing into a human being.

Definitions of emotional/psychological abuse vary from country to country, but the more relevant will be listed and described further in this book and how it can lead adults to attach to narcissistic personalities that continue the cycle of emotional abuse.

Behaviors that can applied to children that classify as emotional/psychological abuse are as follows:

-Rejection: If a child misbehaves, makes a mistake, or expresses pride in an accomplishment, a parent or guardian could use rejection as a tool to belittle or insult the child's lack of abilities or intelligence.

-Isolation: The adult takes the child away from average social experiences and prevents them from forming meaningful bonds.

-Verbally assaulting: The parent or guardian humiliates, name-calls, threats, or insults the child on a consistent basis.

-Negative Comparisons: The adult compares the behavior of the child to that of another negative experience, leading the child to believe that they cannot do anything right.

-Limiting physical contact/affection: Rejecting a child's advances for physical affection makes them feel unloved and unwanted. This may also effect the way the child interprets rejection and physical love throughout the experience of their adult relationships.

-Exposing a child to violence: Oftentimes when a child is being abused, other forms of abuse exist within the household. It is child abuse when a parent or guardian intentionally or unintentionally exposes a minor to acts of violence in their own domestically abusive relationships.

-Using the child as a pawn in relationships: This occurs during or after a divorce between two adults. One parent may apply guilt or shame onto a child when they chose to spend a certain amount of time with one parent, and utilize the silent treatment, rejection, and the limiting of affection in order to punish them for this behavior. This unfortunately is a common occurrence amongst divorced parents. This can cause immense anxiety and demeaned self-worth in a child's mind.

Elder Abuse: The World Health organization defines elder abuse as a "[7]single, or repeated act, inappropriate action that occurs within any relationship where there is an expectation of trust and causes harm to an older person."

Elder abuse is a re-occurring, all-encompassing term that is applied whenever older individuals are taken advantage of and injured physically, psychologically, financially, sexually, and neglected. There is very data gathered that indicates the exact number of older individuals who are being abused, but according to [8]*Elder Abuse Ontario*, 2 to 10 percent of older adults will experience elder abuse in North America in a given year.

There are various forms of abuse that connotes elder abuse, and the main four are listed and described here:

1. Financial Abuse: This is the most common form of elder abuse. This is likely because it often is perpetrated upon the elder by someone who is known to them, such as children,

---

[7] http://www.elderabuseontario.com/what-is-elder-abuse/
[8] http://www.elderabuseontario.com/what-is-elder-abuse/

spouses, or caregivers. Financial abuse occurs when there is direct theft and forgery, using the older person's home without permission or financial balance, or apply inappropriate pressure to the older person to give the permission, sign legal documents that do not understand, or to give items to the abusers.

2. Emotional/psychological Abuse: As described previously, emotional/psychological abuse is any action or verbal cue that degrades a person's self-worth. This can occur to any person of any age, with the abuser falling under any category of age and class. In the realm of elder abuse specifically, threats of institutionalization are used systematically, as well as the act of withholding access to grandchildren. Name-calling, removing the elder's ability to make their own decisions, and forcing isolation are also damaging forms of emotional/psychological abuse toward an elder.

3. Physical Abuse: Physical abuse against elder's is any act that causes physical pain or discomfort. Abusers can be children of the elders, caregivers, or spouses. There have been many unfortunate cases of elder abuse within care homes and nursing facilities. Physical abuse is the most common form of abuse that has been reported to occur in these institutions. Abusers may hit, shove, poke, tie restraints too tightly, burn cigarettes on an elder person, or even spit on them. According

to [9]*Long-Term Care Ombudsman* programs in 2003, there were over 20,000 complaints of abuse from inside nursing homes.

4. Sexual Abuse: Sexual abuse of seniors occurs when an unwanted and unconsented sexual and/or verbal act is performed on an older individual. Sexual abuse of seniors can range from performing forced intercourse, to inappropriate touching and fondling, to coercing nudity for the sake of masturbation or explicit photographing. Those elders who are the most at risk are usually in nursing homes, and observed by a single primary caregiver, who is 81% of the time the abuser. Abusers look for the most vulnerable of seniors so they can avoid repercussions for their actions. According to [10]*Nursing Home Abuse Guide,* only 30% of victims of elder sexual abuse actual report it due to embarrassment and shame.

5. Neglect: Neglect occurs when the basic needs of the older person are not met. Neglect can either appear as intentional, or unintentional. Intentional neglect is when a caregiver intentionally does not meet the needs of the older adult as means of punishment or cruelty. Unintentional neglect is when the needs of the older adult is not met out of carelessness or lack of awareness in how to meet these basic needs. Neglect occurs when a caregiver withholds various

---

[9] https://www.nursinghomeabusecenter.com/elder-abuse/statistics/
[10] http://www.nursinghomeabuseguide.org/sexual-abuse/

services from the elder, leaves the person in a place that is not safe, does not properly deliver medication, or provide basic hygiene, food or water to the individual.

The effects are elder abuse are similar to the general results of domestic and child abuse. If you suspect abuse, it is best to observe the behavior of the individual, such as a sudden onset of depression and anxiety, self-abuse, substance use, and behaviors that are specific results of the kind of abuse the individual suffered. If you suspect that someone you know, or even if you, whether it be an adult, child, or senior is being abused, keep an eye open for these specific signs and symptoms:

Domestic Abuse:

-Expressing fearfulness of partner. You or a friend may be afraid to express a different opinion or to express yourself to your partner, just in case it diverts from what your partner believes is correct.

-You or someone you know partner controls them financially, socially.

-A partner makes constant threats of violence or embarrassment.

-A partner makes inappropriate jokes or comments about their partner in public.

-Insults and belittles you or a friend on how they look and/or level of intelligence.

-A partner forces sex or sexual acts on you or a friend when you've already turned them down.

-The appearance of bruises and the attempt to hide them.

-Sudden absences.

-Character changes through the presence of depression and anxiety.

Child Abuse:

-Withdrawing from friends or social activities.

-Changes in school performances.

-Appearance of bruises, broken limbs.

-Sexual knowledge or behavior that is inappropriate for the child's age.

-Low-confidence and self-esteem.

-Defiant and anti-social behavior.

-Stunted growth.

-Poor hygiene.

-Constantly seeking food.

-Behaviors in parents or caregivers could express intense lack of interest in the child's well-being, a constant blaming of the child for problems, describing the child in negative terms, and applying harsh discipline upon the child in the presence of other people.

Elder Abuse:

-The elder may behave withdrawn.

-The elder expresses the sudden onset of depression/anxiety.

-The elder expresses fear of the most consistent Care giver.

-The elder may have trouble sleeping.

-The elder may refuse suddenly to take medication.

-Withdrawals from bank accounts may appear and are unexplainable.

-Legal documents suddenly disappear.

-The elder may display an unkempt physical appearance, such as messy hair, skin rashes, long toenails, or have bedsores.

If any of these forms of abuse are suspected, it would be best to contact someone of whom you trust to express your concerns and make an action plan with.

Chapter 2: Emotional/Psychological Abuse: Diving Deeper

"The narcissist inflicts pain and abuse on others. He devalues Sources of Supply, callously and off-handedly abandons them, and discards people, places, partnerships, and friendships unhesitatingly. Sudden shifts between sadism and altruism, abuse and 'love', ignoring and caring, abandoning and clinging, viciousness and remorse, the harsh and the tender - are, perhaps, the most difficult to comprehend and to accept. These swings produce in people around the narcissist emotional insecurity, an eroded sense of self worth, fear, stress, and anxiety ('walking on eggshells'). Gradually, emotional paralysis ensues and they come to occupy the same emotional wasteland inhabited by the narcissist, his prisoners and hostages in more ways than one - and even when he is long out of their life. "

Article: Other People's Pain by Sam Vaknin
http://www.suite101.com/article.cfm/npd/76632

As discussed in the previous chapter, emotional/psychological abuse is any form of action, whether it be verbal, physical, or technological, that diminishes a person's self-worth, self-esteem, confidence, and connection to their reality and grip on sanity. We explored the many manifestations of abuse and their emotional/psychological component. For the rest of this book, an emphasis will be placed further on the behaviors that fall under the category of emotional/psychological abuse as it occurs in domestic relationships, with children, and the elderly. This form of abuse is the kind that is often difficult to identify and define, especially when physical and sexual abuse are absent. This chapter will dive deeper into the behaviors that fall under the category of emotional/psychological abuse and the various mental health effects that occur when falling victim to these horrible acts. Emotional/psychological abuse is usually subtler and tactical when applied on a consistent basis.

The Many Faces of Emotional/Psychological Abuse

Anyone can fall victim to an emotional/psychological abuser. Abusers are not always romantic partners. They can be mothers and fathers, aunts and uncles, fellow siblings, authority figures, co-workers, bosses, caregivers, and even peers at school. In this section, the prevalece of emotional/psychological abuse and specific tactics that abusers apply depending upon the victim's relationship to the abuser will be explored. As previously stated, it is crucial to continue to emphasize that most of the time abusers know their victim well, which utilizes the notion of trust to their benefit.

1. Children: Adult to Child Relationships

Most cases of child mistreatment generally involve a parental figure, according the the [11]CIS. In 82% of the cases collected, one parent was the main perpetrator. 56% of the time, the abusers were father/step-fathers/common-in-law partners, whereas 66% were mothers/stepmothers/common-law partners in relation to sole emotionally abusive tactics. It is rare that an individual will be investigated for emotional/psychological abuse alone, as it is generally physical or exposure to domestic abuse that substantiates eventual investigation. The *2003 Canadian incidence Study of Reported Child Abuse and Neglect* found that emotional/psychological abuse of children was associated with all other forms of abuse, i.e. neglect, physical, sexual, and exposure to partner domestic violence.

2. Men and women: Heterosexual Relationships

A 2004 General Social Survey noted that emotional/psychological abuse was 2.5 times more common in heterosexual relationships than physical abuse. The report was almost equal amongst men and women who noted emotional/psychologically abusive behaviors; 17% of men and

---

[11] https://www.canada.ca/en/public-health/services/health-promotion/stop-family-violence/prevention-resource-centre/family-violence/psychological-abuse-discussion-paper.html

18% of women reported experiencing this form of abuse from their partners. Although the study found these numbers to be strikingly similar, it was also found that over time the effects of emotional/psychological abuse were more prolonged amongst women then men. The most common forms of this kind of abuse reported were name-calling, the expression of jealousy, and the assertion to know exactly who the partner was with during an outing.

Majority of the studies that have been conducted on emotional/psychological abuse have been on couples who are heterosexual. Here, the most common forms of emotional/psychological abuse found within these studies will be defined in order to help identify abusive behaviors that may appear hidden to the abused.

-**Gas lighting**: This is a common tactic that abusers apply to their victims in order to make their partner feel like they cannot trust their own reality. This occurs when an abuser constantly denies something that the victim claims they did or said, or something that you say happened to you. The goal is for you, as the victim, to begin questioning your own memory, and to rely solely on your partner as the source for 'the truth'. The victim will begin to only rely on the partner as an external source, which always them to be further manipulated and controlled. Extreme examples of this behavior is catching tangible evidence that a

34

spouse may be being unfaithful, but the cheating spouse denies it, which directly doubts the victim's perception of reality and sense reality. The term is derived from a play of the same title by Patrick Hamilton, that told the story of an abusive husband who manipulated her physical environment and then convinced her that she was imagining those changes.

Gas lighting as a tactic is believed to have contributed to the sexist notion of women being 'too sensitive, jealous, paranoid' and more inclined toward self-doubt. The goal is for the victim not to trust themselves, their thoughts, beliefs, and perceptions. Although this tactic is most often applied by men to women in a heterosexual relationship, it can still occur the opposing way, as well as in same-sex relationships, parents to children, older-children to parents, and adult authority figures to children. The first step toward recovery is recognizing how you feel as a victim and to seek out the aid of someone you trust who isn't your partner. If you believe something has occurred, or things have occurred in the past that your partner is denying and you are beginning to question your own mental health, then this is the best time to reach out.

-Victim Blaming: This behavior essentially throws the responsibility of the abuser onto the abused and blames the victim for their outrageous behavior. The abuser will focus on the notion that had their victim just behaved the way they wanted

Cycle of Abuse

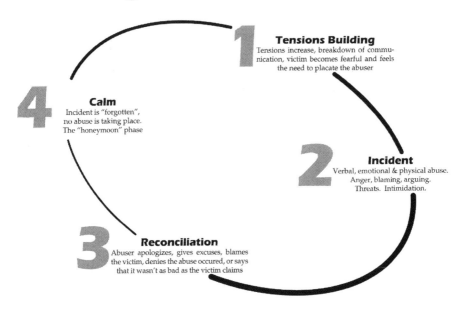

1 Tensions Building
Tensions increase, breakdown of communication, victim becomes fearful and feels the need to placate the abuser

4 Calm
Incident is "forgotten", no abuse is taking place. The "honeymoon" phase

2 Incident
Verbal, emotional & physical abuse. Anger, blaming, arguing. Threats. Intimidation.

3 Reconciliation
Abuser apologizes, gives excuses, blames the victim, denies the abuse occured, or says that it wasn't as bad as the victim claims

them to, situation X would not have happened. This form of abuse can be sexual, physical, emotional/psychological. Even when the victim is being abused, according to the abuser, their behavior is the fault of the victim's. For example, if an abuser hits their partner for not having dinner ready at the appropriate time, it would be the victim's fault for not having dinner ready on time. It is important to emphasize that the behavior of an abuser is never the victim's fault. This tactic simply is another method of degrading the victim's self-worth.

-The Emotionally Abusive Cycle: All forms of abuse follow the same general cycle of abuse, and then there are sub-format of how specific kinds of abuse cycle themselves around. Emotional abuse as previously stated is harder for a victim to identify. Unless the behavior is observed by close friends and family, or the victim is able to reach out for help, the cycle will continue repeating itself. There is always tension building, and then, in the case of emotional/psychological abuse, an argument may erupt where the abuser uses threats, name-calling, gas lighting or other psychological tactics in order to bring their victim down. Reconciliation occurs in the form of apologies and/or gifts, and things seem calm for a while. But is certain that the abuser's behavior will continue around and around this cycle, making the emotionally abused person's experience of abuse long and arduous.

-Isolation: Making sure that their victim does not have many close friends or family members help the abuser maintain his/her/their hold on the individual they are abusing. The abuser will constantly check where their victim is going, who they are seeing, and go to extraordinary efforts to isolate them from those their victim trusts most. This behavior is often noticed by outside family members first. Isolation allows the abusers to control the victim and their behavior. It is through the abrupt change of people who once socialized often with friends or family who suddenly become absent that this form of abuse is taken notice of.

This would be a good time for loved one to inquire to the person they care about whether or not their partner is making outing decisions for them. Or, making them believe that the outing is not worth their time through manipulation.

3. Same-sex Relationships

The same tactics are applied by abusers in same-sex relationships as they are in heterosexuell ones, studies confirm. But due to the societal stigma of homosexuality, not as many studies have been done on the entire experience of abuse with same-sex couples. But there is one particular tactic that is unique to same-sex couple emotional/psychological abuse; the constant threat of being outed.

Depending where the couple is living, the concept of having a partner that is your same-sex could be dangerous fact to be shared with family, employers, and even lawmakers. Direct threats are made to out their partner in order to exert continuous control over them. Homosexual individuals feel a deep sense of fear if they do not disclose their orientation to certain people in their lives, therefore, they allow their abusive partner to hold this above this heads. It is also less likely within the LGBTQ plus community that an abused person will seek help due to a perceived bias of their sexuality or gender. Lesbian women were noted in a [12]2002 study as being unable to locate services to deal with anger or control issues due to their orientation. The same emotionally-abusive tactics are applied in same-sex relationships, but enhanced with the looming threat of having their orientation exposed to people the victim does not want to be made aware of.

4. Peer-Relationships: Child-to-Child (Bullying)

Emotionally/psychologically abusive relationships that occur between children is known as bullying. Bullying has become an increasing concern over time as social media continues to thrive in popularity. Bullying can occur in person physically and emotionally, and is engaged through fighting/striking, and name-calling and rumor spreading. Social media bullying is generally focused on the notion of false rumors and virtual name-calling. A Canadian study conducted in 2004 found 18% of girls and 25% of boys acted as the abuser from grades 6-10. The same study found 21% of girls and 25% of boys reported themselves as being the victim of their abuse. Boys tend to rely on a physical form of bullying, such as punching and fighting. Young females use word tactics to 'gossip' about classmates. While the term abuser is somewhat new in relation to bullying in children, it still stands as accurate. When the bully is applying their tactics, whether it be

---

[12] Sense man 2002, 27-32; Walters, Simoni and Horwath 2001, 147

verbal, physical, or virtually through social media, the goal is to control and exert power over someone they perceive as being weak. Bullying behavior as minors is easier to grow out of and develop from, especially if the abuser is of a younger age. It is best to deter this behavior immediately in hopes of preventing another abusing adult to grow up and continue using those around them for their benefit.

5. Authority Figures Who Abuse

This section will focus on the various forms of abuse that occur between victims and individuals who hold a position of power over them. Abusers can act as coaches, teachers, caregivers, and employers. Any of these individuals are capable of other forms of abuse as well, such as physical and sexual, due to their ability to take advantage of individuals who consider them an important figure in their lives.

Caregivers can take care of the elderly, the physically or mentally disabled, and children. Emotional and/or psychological abuse is applied in order for rules to be followed, i.e., in order to control those of whom they feel are inferior to them. Some caregivers who abuse may feel like those of whom they are supposedly 'caring' for are not at the same level of cognitive ability of them, and therefore do not deserve be treated with the same respect. [13]A study

---

[13] Curry, Hassouneh-Phillips and Johnston-Silverberg 2001, 70-71

conducted in Canada in 2001 found that the more women with disabilities depended on a person to care for them, the more likely they were to be exposed to emotional/psychological abuse.

Teachers often mesh together the notion of discipline along with emotionally/psychologically abusive behavior in order to validate their actions. Children are often name-called and insulted in order to be 'kept in line' by their educators. School-time experiences with teachers who emotionally/psychologically abused a child often stay with them and contribute to low self-esteem, low self-confidence, and low academic self-esteem.

Coaches who emotionally/psychologically abuse their athletes is the most legitimized more of abuse listed in this book. Name-calling, harassment, insults and threatening tactics are applied in order to 'motivate' the athlete into a better performance. A Canadian study in 2000 though did note how the behaviors of a coach toward their athletes can be carried down toward fellow athletes, the opposing team, and even the original coach who abused them. Many young athletes who have been emotionally/psychologically abused have noted lower confidence, feelings of worthlessness, anger and fear. It is also significantly harder for male athletes to report feelings of abuse due to stigma in sport and the perception of masculinity.

6. The Elderly

This book previously focused on the various forms of emotional/psychologically abuse that the elderly is susceptible to. This form of abuse is the most common amongst the elderly, and like in domestic relationships, is one of the hardest to recognize due to the vulnerability of the victim. There are several tactics the are easier to carry out on an elderly victim, especially if their physical/mental state is in decline.

Sometimes children emotionally/psychologically abuse their elderly parents. An abuser may threaten them with punishment of deprivation, which delays the giving of food, water, and medication, as well as placing needed object father away than the elderly person can reach. The abuser applies insults, name-calling, and other forms of threats in order to control the older individual. The elderly is often treated like children by their abuser, especially when within a care home. Although Todays Geriatric Medicine reports that 90% of those who abuse the elderly are their family members, there is still reason to question a caregiver should an elderly family member display abrupt displays of depression/anxiety and diminishing self-care, as well as other signs and symptoms which will be described in further detail in the next section of our chapter.

Effects of Emotional/Psychological Abuse

The effect that emotional/psychological abuse can have on an individual varies vastly and is dependent upon many contributing factors. All emotional/psychological abuse has an effect, but the severity and longevity of the effects depend upon the following differentiating elements: age of abuse, gender/relation of abuser, severity and longevity of the abuse and the path or attempted path taken toward healing. For the sake of this book, the disorders that are likely to develop due to the experience of emotional/psychological abuse as well as statistically relevant age and gender relations will be described.

Post Traumatic Stress Disorder: PTSD is a mental health diagnosis that includes a cluster of symptoms all placed under the same category. The experience of PTSD is different for every person, but there is one aspect of the disorder that all sufferers have in common; it is triggered by a severely traumatic or life-threatening event, the occurrence of multiple traumatizing events. In the case of abuse, particularly, emotional/psychological abuse, trauma is a built up, daily occurrence, that takes longer to detect than physical or sexual abuse.

Psychiatrist experts have created three categories of PTSD symptoms that fall under either the re-experiencing of the

43

dramatic event(s), avoidance of reminders of the tragic event, and responses of hyper arousal. Not every person will experience the same symptoms in quantity or frequency. Some of the most common symptoms are listed here as follows:

—An intense feeling of stress when recalling event(s).
—An intense physical reaction when reminded of event(s) such as sweating, heart palpitations, nausea.
—Upsetting memories arising.
—Lost of interest in life activities.
—Detachment from others.
—Avoiding activities that remind them of said event(s).
—Difficulty with memory of traumatic event(s).

The following are descriptions of the effects of emotional/psychological abuse dependent upon age range of abuse experienced. The symptoms of PTSD and other psychiatric disorders are particular to emotional/psychological abuse, based upon a 2002 Canadian study conducted by [14]EKOS Research Associates, where the attitude toward family violence was being observed.

---

[14] https://www.canada.ca/en/public-health/services/health-promotion/stop-family-violence/prevention-resource-centre/family-violence/psychological-abuse-discussion-paper.html

Children (Infancy to age 12):

—Elevated level of cortisol (a hormone secreted during stressful events) This occurrence has been estimated to affect the area of the brain that is important for memory formation.

—Higher risk of being bullied.

—Language delays.

—Overt aggression.

—Indirect aggression; spreading gossip.

—Social withdrawal, difficulty making friends.

Adolescents (Age 13-19):

—PTSD in both male and female victims.

—Expression of emotional/psychological abuse toward dating partners.

—Poor performance in school.

—Depression and withdrawal from social events.

—Arrival of eating disorders and self-mutilation (more common with female victims.)

—Arrival of the abuse of drugs and alcohol (more likely for male victims.)

—Suicide attempts or ideation in both male and female victims.

Adults (Age 20-64):

—The experience of PTSD likely for both men and women.

—Sensations of shame and guilt.

—Depression and withdrawal.

—Abuse of drugs and alcohol.

—Suicide attempts.

—Risk-taking behavior dependent upon gender.

Elderly (Age 65 and up):

—Signs of PTSD in both female and male.

—Fear and anxiety around caregiver/children.

—Learned helplessness.

—Exhibit behavior that are often associated with dementia, and is misdiagnosed as dementia; rocking, sucking, biting, etc.)

—Depression.

—Low self-esteem.

—Anger.

—Self-harm.

—Issues of insomnia.

—Loss of appetite unrelated to medical issues.

—Substance abuse, usually alcohol.

Enabling: A Form of Secondary Abuse?

Enabling is defined as behavior that allows other negative behavior to pervade. Enabling is a term that is often associated with psychological disorders or issues, such as substance abuse and various forms of abuse. In terms of emotional/ psychological abuse, there are two particular forms of enabling that allow the abuser to continue apply their controlling tactics. In one case, the person is conscious and aware of the abuse occurring and does nothing to stop it, and in another, is a person who has fallen under the spell of the narcissist's behaviors and may be a victim of gas lighting themselves.

1. Direct Enabling: Observation of emotional/psychological abuse is not as easy as the observation of physical or sexual abuse. Nevertheless, it is still possible for a person to detect when behavior of the abused becomes altered over time. For example, a sister could notice how her usually sociable sister, who likes to go out to the bar with her friends most weekends, abruptly stops doing this. She may also notice absences with or without explanation, fear and anxiety around their partner/abuser, as well as an inability to speak for themselves. A direct form of enabling is when a person notices something is wrong but does not to raise the issue to the abuser or the abused. This is generally a close friend or family member in martial situations. The person uses the overused excuse of wanting to 'mind their own business' when their loved one is being abused. This can be seen as a form of secondary abuse as it is the silence of loved ones who are in a position of existing outside the manipulator's control and still choose to stand back.

2. Unconscious Enabling: This form of enabling in abusive situations is far less culpable because the person is also a victim of a narcissist's abusive tactics. (The particulars of a narcissistic personality and link toward abusive behavior will be explored in the next chapter.) For example, if an adult child is emotionally/psychologically abusing their elderly parent, they could also be gaslighting their own siblings or spouse in order to hide the abuse from their loved one. It is also likely that this person is vulnerable to their emotionally abusive tactics and is not aware themselves of the behavior involved that is keeping them on the cycle of continuous abuse.

This is also an opportune time to discuss the notion of supposed unconditional love in domestic relationships and how it can act as a self-enabler in abusive relationships.

Many people, particularly women in heterosexual relationships, have been fed the notion over time that they must love their partner unconditionally. In some cases, this involves standing by your partner when they continue abusing you, staying within the cycle whether it be emotionally, physically or sexually, out of the dedication of 'love'. This self-rationalization for the acceptance of unruly behavior is a fallacy, and a form of self-enabling in abusive relationships. It is important to emphasize here that abuse is never the fault of the abused; but the abuse can be enabled when the excuse of unconditional love is brought into the equation.

Unconditional love does not involve abuse. Unconditional love in no examples has ever acted as the remedy to cure the abuser of their controlling and manipulative ways. The only way that an abuser can be halted is to end the relationship, or to cut off ties with the abuser entirely. Counselling is possible for the abuser, but cannot involve any of their victims. The cycle is always going to continue, no matter how much love the abused believes they can give the abuser.

When the Church is Abusive

When a person is engaged in the faith of the Catholic Church, it is often a place they turn when experiencing turmoil in their lives. It is often thought of as a place of solace, where they could confide in a pastor with some of their most painful experiences. But according to Dr. David Hawkins of the Christian Broadcast Network, this reality is often a fallacy within the church walls.

In an article written in 2018, Hawkins talks about how the church needs to develop more modern tactics in approaching those who seek help and comfort when they are being abused. It is common for the church to act as a secondary emotional abuser when informing the victim that they must pray more, or that it is only

God who can judge their abuser, whether it be a partner or authority figure. These behaviors are invalidating, and do nothing to aid the individual in removing themselves from the abusive situation and beginning a journey of healing.

Hawkins makes 7 different suggestions can help bring Church services into the modern age and help those out who are the victims of emotional/psychological abuse:

1. Validation: Applying active listening skills when an abuse victim is describing their story. Validating emotions helps the victim feel like they are being heard.
2. Interest: Show that you and the church community care about how the victim is being ill-treated. This will give the victim a self-confidence their abuser may have greatly diminished in them.
3. Educate: Church staff could begin educating themselves on the various forms of abuse and the tactics that narcissistic personalities apply in order to maintain control over their victim. More awareness also validates the emotions of the abused.
4. Measure the danger: Take note of how severe the case of abuse is and make an action plan to help the individual begin to severe the ties from their abuser.

5. Connect: Connecting the victim to other counsellors and services that are specific to abuse will help them on their way toward healing.

6. Hold accountability: Encourage the victim to seek counselling and asset that no form of abuse is their fault as the victim. It is up to abuser to hold themselves accountable for their behavior, and their behavior alone.

7. Give Visibility: By developing an open discussion on emotional/psychological abuse as well as other forms of abuse, the church could act as a leader and open the doors for other victims to stand up for themselves or to begin seeking the help they require. This also helps the church to appear more modern and statistically aware of the issues in modern society, rather than running from them.

There are also cases of direct psychological abuse that involves the church on its own. This form of abuse has been termed religious abuse, and could stand on its own plain as another form of abuse using various methods of other abuse to sustain it. These actions can be categorized as abuse against children, physical abuse, religious violence, spiritual abuse, and psychological abuse.

Psychological abuse within the church occurs when the teachings of a religion are used to inflict emotional/psychological harm upon another person. The abuser is generally in the position of authority within the same or similar faith as the abused. This form of abuse can be well-intentioned or ill-intentioned. Tactics used by those in authority use and distort the word of their particular faith in order to make a person behave in a certain way, in the name of their religion. A common example is the avoidance of medical treatment, and to apply prayer instead. This form of abuse usually effects children and vulnerable adults more, especially when many of the teachings of the faith are taken too literally. Victims of this abuse have reported feelings of anxiety, depression, and the development of phobias that are specific to their religious affiliation. For example, a child may feel so intensely guilted by the act of stealing a toy from school, confides in a religious figure for comfort, and is scolded for the act. This sensation of guilt applied in the name of religion is a form of emotional/psychological abuse.

Shame is also a common emotion experienced by those who have felt emotionally/psychologically abused by their church. Even if they chose to depart from the faith, shame and guilt toward a certain belief or behavior continues to stay with them as adults. This form of abuse is engaged in in the name of religion or a certain faith, and is thus harder to notice by the victim due to their observation of the pastor or church figure as the wise one.

Religion can also be used as a useful tool amongst those who emotionally/psychologically abuse their partners, children, parents, or the elderly. Religion as a moral compass and source of self-understanding, embeds itself deep within the abused when used correctly as an abusive tool, and is thus makes it harder to break the abusive cycle. For example, a male and a female may be devout Christians, and therefore, do not believe in intercourse before marriage. But this may have occurred before the couple became married, so the abuser can use this as a tool to keep control over his partner by inducing guilt and shame. Other forms of religious abuse could appear as so:

—Prevention of practicing religious beliefs: Partners, family members or friends may practice different religions, but the abuser always wants to assert control. The abuser will not allow their victim to practice their religion because it is not what they want. They may demand their victim to behave in ways that go against their religion, such as forcing them to eat pork as a Muslim.

—Ridiculing beliefs: Criticism of partners or friends in an emotionally/psychologically abusive manner occurs often in abusive relationships. But when someone is religious, it adds fuel to the abuser's fire because they have something personal and specific that they can use against you, and continue to claim that you are 'too oversensitive'.

—Using your beliefs to criticize: If you are Christian and do not believe in attending church services consistently, the abuser may use their victim's lack of appearance at service as a way to label them as a 'heathen' or claim they are 'going to hell'. These kind of accusations can cause great feelings of shame and guilt for the victim of the abuse.

—Using religion to manipulate behavior: The methods that the abuser applies are now being done in the name of your or their religion. They may use random bible scripture in order to assert their dominance or to create a more deeply felt sense of guilt when a victim's behavior does not directly align with strict religious teachings.

—Validation of abuse: If a person is strictly religious, it is easy for an abuser to use something that is close to their heart to validate their behavior and further encourage the cycle of abuse. If someone says something in the bible that is verbally or emotionally abusive, the abuser may use this as validation in order for them to participate in their own version of seed abuse. For example, pressuring the victim into being a homemaker in a heterosexual relationship and using the bible as an excuse is a commonly noted act. Telling the victim that they will be spited if they are found out to be lying because it is a sin is another act of religious abuse that could occur.

In any matter, using something that is so faceted as religion in order to maintain control over another individual merely speaks to the all-encompassing nature of a narcissistic personality and their lack of empathy. Abuse is not something that thrives outside the walls of various institutions; religions all over the world as used as effective tools to keep the vulnerable under control. If the church is a congregation that continuously suggests praying or further validates the person's behavior as a flawed being, it is time to either seek further psychological aid. Further aid can also be sought out within other congregations of the same faith who understand the modern reality of emotional/psychological abuse.

If you feel that someone you love or care about is being emotionally/psychologically abused by the church, or an individual in their life is using religion as a tool of manipulation, it would be fruitful to contact their congregation and ask about their approach to the situation. Any person who stands by and allows the abuse are simply enabling the situation, whether it be intentional or unintentional. The church certainly acts within the capacity as well, and is not immune to the fallacy of unconditional love in abusive relationships.

Chapter 3: Narcissism and the Diagnosis' of Abusers

"Don't worry, he didn't pick you because you are weak or an easy target. He picked you because you have all the qualities he wants and can't have. The problem Is, while he was, as we say, sucking you dry he caused you over time to feel confused, edgy, distracted and all the things you described. We loved these men and why wouldn't we? In the beginning they make us feel so special and comfortable and loved. It's later when, like you described, our minds are reeling because we know something Is 'off but can't put our fingers on It that we start searching around and find ourselves here. Then all the pieces start to fall in to place. People with NDP are master manipulators, subtle and strong at the same time. You have been brainwashed and It's going to take a while to detox but you'll be all right. It's Important not to blame yourself but get on with detaching both physically and mentally. Not easy and not pleasant."

So far we have explored the various characteristics and personality traits of individuals who are susceptible to emotional/psychological abuse. But what is the person who does the abusing like? What kind of traits should people look out for to not land themselves in an abusive situation? In this chapter, the definition of a narcissistic abuser will be deeply explored and examined, as well as other mental health diagnoses' that some abusers fall under. The psychology of the narcissistic abuser and what drives them toward their specific victim will also be discussed.

Allow this chapter to be your guide toward detecting the traits of a person who may be emotionally/psychologically abusing you, a loved one, a child around you, employees at work, or a parent. This chapter delves into the statistical relevance of personalities that tend to abuse, but it is important to remember that anyone with any previous mental health diagnoses can be an abuser, just as much as the fact that not every abuser has a mental health diagnoses.

What is a Narcissistic Personality?

The word 'narcissist' comes from a story in Greek mythology, where Narcissus fell in love with his own image. The narcissistic personality is defined as a person who idealized their own self-image and attributes to the point of negatively effected other people's lives. Many people have possessed narcissistic traits when it has to do with a certain section of their lives, but also possess a healthy dose of humility and self-doubt. This is not the case for a person with a narcissistic personality.

In 2004, psychiatrists Hotchkiss and James F. Masterson listed what they called the [15]*Seven Deadly Sins of Narcissism:*

1. Shamelessness: Narcissists do not express feeling shame for any behavior or belief they may possess, as the sensation of feeling shame implies that they must have done something wrong.

2. Magical Thinking: A psychological defense mechanism that allows them to see themselves as flawless, and project shame onto others rather than feel it themselves.

3. Envy: A narcissist may employ the feeling of contempt toward another person in order to avoid feelings of jealousy in reaction to the result of another person's achievements.

4. Arrogance: A narcissist likes to raise their own self-importance by degrading others.

5. Entitlement: Believing that they are special and deserve special treatment, and begin expressing narcissistic rage they are denied it (a reaction when a threat to their self-worth is perceived).

6. Exploitation: The narcissist may employ exploitation without regard for the feelings of others. This is usually done to another person who is in a position of subservience and

---

[15] Hotchkiss, Sandy & Masterson, James F. Why Is It Always About You? : The Seven Deadly Sins of Narcissism (2003)

cannot escape it, such as in a work setting, or chidden at school.

7. Lack of /bad boundaries: Boundaries simply do not exist for a person who is a full-blown narcissist. They are unaware that other people can exist not solely to suit their needs, and that other people may have different thoughts or feelings than themselves. Narcissistic supply is a term used to describe how narcissist rely on codependents in order to fill their sense of self-worth.

Narcissistic Personality Disorder (NPD)

NPD is a personality disorder that expresses a long-term pattern of behavior that is self-focused, superior, exploitative of others and severely lacks empathy for others. The difference between NPD and the previously described traits of a person with a narcissistic personality is the consistency of the traits and to what extent they impair their lives. This difference, is described as pathological; when the expression of these traits consistently disrupt the lives of the narcissist is when a mental health diagnoses is given. Many people possess narcissistic personality traits and are able to live a successful and stress-free life, while those with NPD may perceive themselves this way, are actually not developing and achieving success due to the crippling fear of criticism, self-doubt, and failure that lies under their inflated sense of self worth.

The M'alignant Narcissist

These kind of narcissists are ones that are not bothered by guilt, and has the ability to resemble antisocial personality disorder. APD is another personality disorder defined primarily by antisocial behavior that has no consideration for right and wrong. The malignant narcissist may take pleasure in causing pain and display forms of sadistic behavior. The key difference though between a malignant narcissist and an antisocial personality is the way the person relates to others. Narcissists share a codependent relationship with others, and deep down, require the approval of others in order to function. A person with antisocial personality disorder could not care less about the opinion of others, and do not require the engagement of other people in order to feel validated.

The Narcissist and Emotional/Psychological Abuse: What Truly Lies Beneath

Abuse is the behavioral act that a narcissist applies as a defense mechanism against a variety of emotions that the narcissist is constantly attempting to suppress. Despite the outward expression of self-importance, grandiosity, lacking of empathy, and cruel behavior, the narcissist is actually acting out of deeply repressed sensations of fear. They fear rejection, their own imperfections and shortcomings, of being abandoned, unwanted and unloved.

The following section will summarize 14 behavioral expressions of a narcissist and how it connects to being abusive. A narcissist could be an authority figure, a parent, a partner, a teacher, a coach, or a caregiver. Marjalis Fjelstad writes about the behaviors to look out for if you believe someone in your life is a narcissist on [16]*Mind Body Green.*

1. Narcissists feel the need to the be the best/most at everything in their lives. Even if it means the sickest, or injured, they must be at the top

2. A narcissist constantly feels the need to acquire validation from a partner or important person in their lives because they subconsciously believed that they are not good enough. External validation is always required, but never enough. They will always want you to praise them because they cannot provide the confidence and assuredly for themselves, despite the outward appearance of confidence and egotism.

3. Narcissists are perfectionists, which means they those that are in their lives must be perfect, they must be perfect, and

---

[16] https://www.mindbodygreen.com/articles/14-signs-of-narcissism

everything that they have planned or envisioned for themselves must play out without a hitch. This, of course is not how life works, which often leads to the narcissist feeling dissatisfied. Perfectionism is why it is endlessly difficult for a narcissist to receive any criticism, even if it is constructive.

4. Because of the perfectionism, narcissist want to control everything around them, which includes a partner, a child, a parent, etc. This is where control in abusive relationships comes from, because the behavior of the victim is not lining up with the exact ways the abuser wants it to.

5. Narcissists never take responsibility for their actions. Even if they contributed to the not so flawless way something may have been carried about, the fault is never their own, it is yours, because you did do exactly as you were instructed. Noting they ever do can be wrong.

6. As preciously stated, narcissist cannot comprehend what boundaries are. They cannot comprehend that you have your own thoughts, feelings, expectations, and past. They do not like when another person expresses feelings that oppose their own, because it is not perfect, which leads to more behaviors that attempt to control their entire world.

7. The narcissist lacks empathy, which is why they are unable to understand boundaries. They cannot correctly read body language or facial expressions because they believe that other people must feel the same way they do. But they are also overly sensitive and aware of perceived rejection from others,

and constantly believe that the source of their negative feelings are caused by the person they are closest to in their life.

8. Logic does not work with the narcissist. Trying to explain to a narcissist how their behavior effects you is futile, because they are only aware of their own thoughts and feelings.

9. Splitting is a term used to describe how narcissists categorize every feeling, person and experience into one of two categories; the good and the bad. This is due to their intense sense of perfectionism. Nothing can be a combination of a positively valence experience and a negatively perceived one. They can only cope with the single experience that is their own.

10. An appearance of surety and self-confidence hide the narcissist true experience of fear; fear of failure, losing money, their partner leaving them, their children being taken away, etc. No matter how close a person can get to a narcissist, they will never be able to build a trusting relationship, simply because the narcissist is in constant fear of being abandonad.

11. Anxiety is a looming sensation for the narcissist, who projects this sensation onto their siblings, partner, or parent. This is not an enjoyable sensation for the narcissist, so they rather throw it onto someone else.

12. Shamelessness may appear to be a trait of the narcissist, but it is truly an expression of the opposite. Shame means that there is something wrong about a person, and the narcissist

cannot cope with this notion. Feeling shame is the enemy, so they do not allow themselves to feel it and bury it deep inside their subconscious. They hate that they possess insecurities and fear, and live with this lingering sensation that becomes projected on the closest loved one who may 'find them out.'

13. Since the narcissist doesn't want to accept that they feel fear or insecurities, they are unable to feel vulnerable. This makes it difficult to create and maintain close intimate relationships. The narcissist is constantly displaying this flawless sense of self-importance and perfection to the point where the true human beneath that is hidden from those that the narcissist considers the most important.

14. Lack of empathy means that the narcissist cannot work or communicante in a group setting, because only their wants,

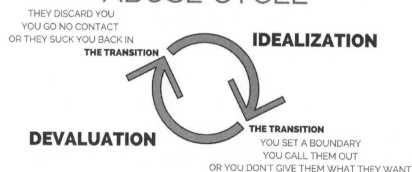

THE NARCISSISTIC
ABUSE CYCLE

THEY DISCARD YOU
YOU GO NO CONTACT
OR THEY SUCK YOU BACK IN
THE TRANSITION

IDEALIZATION

DEVALUATION

THE TRANSITION
YOU SET A BOUNDARY
YOU CALL THEM OUT
OR YOU DON'T GIVE THEM WHAT THEY WANT

needs, and thoughts are what truly exist in their world.

Narcissistic Victim Syndrome: When an Empath Meets a Narcissist

There exists an infinite amount of research and literature on narcissistic personality traits and narcissistic personality disorder, as well as the abuse inflicted upon those who get sucked into cycle of abuse. But within the past decade, an interest in the effects of this form of abuse have arisen, and thus has a specific diagnosis that pertains the narcissistic abuse; narcissistic victim syndrome.

Narcissistic Victim Syndrome (NVS) is defined as a group of symptoms experienced by a person who is closely related to a narcissist. This person could be a child, an adult, or even an elderly person experiencing abuse by a caregiver or their own children. It is a newly discovered term that has very minimal literature associated with it. Clinically it can defined in the Diagnostic and Statistical Manuel (DSM) under C-PTSD (class C of post-traumatic stress disorder).

The experience of this disorder is precisely how a victim feels when they have been emotionally/psychologically abused. It may take years for a victim to realize that they were being abused, and to then seek help for it because it is so unrecognized. [17]Kim Saeed lists 6 signs that may indicate you are suffering from NVS, and therefore, have been dealing with an emotional/psychological abuse committed by a narcissist.

1. Feeling alone: The feeling of being alone is constant. Although your partner or person you care for may be around you, you are constantly wishing that someone will come and comfort you.

2. You aren't enough: Not matter how much success you have achieved in your life, your partner or person in your life does not recognize it, not matter what.

3. Your entire life is the relationship: Other interests, social events and friends have evaporated and almost all of your mental and physical energy is put into 'fixing' or enduring the relationship.

4. You compromise your values: You stop standing up for what you believe in in order to make your partner/abuser content. You have stopped behaving in ways that you feel are valuable, or even started participating in behaviors that they value in the name of 'being in love.' Examples of this are participating in sexual activities you never would have in the past, or you've stopped tipping at restaurants because your abuser disapproves of it.

---

[17] https://kimsaeed.com/2015/10/12/6-strong-signs-you-have-narcissistic-abuse-syndrome/

5. You feel unworthy due to name calling: Name-calling is meant to hurt you, no matter how many times a person in your life may claim that they are 'only joking' and that you are 'too sensitive.' There is nothing about their life that gives them the excuse to demean you, ever.

6. You are exhausted by the cycle of abuse: The constant cycle of abuse relies on the carousel ride of hurt and rescue. The abuser often applies the silent treatment as a tactic, to evoke your fear of abandonment, but then returns, making their victim feel relief. This cycle is repeated over and over again, which further weakens the resolve of the victim, lowering their standards and allowing more inappropriate behavior out of fear of abandonment.

If any of these feelings reside within you, you are dealing with emotional/psychological abuse. Because the diagnosis of the syndrome is so new, treatment options will vary. It is important to recognize that a narcissist is not as easy to identify as is clearly written out in this book. Most narcissists, especially those in domestic relationships, initially appear wonderful; full of charm, excitement, romance, security. It is only when you have been won over that the true hideousness that this person has been hiding will be revealed.

Differences between Other Disorders of similar Nature: The Borderline and Histrionic Personality

Abusive personalities do not always fall under the category of a Narcissistic Personality. There are several other disorders that can be abusive and still manage to follow the cycled pattern of abuse. Here, three of most commonly confused disorders will be discussed and how they relate to patterns of abuse.

It is also important to note that there are gender biases when it comes to certain disorders and their diagnoses, in relation to behavior and how it can often be classified as gender specific. For example, women are more likely to be diagnosed with histrionic personality disorder or borderline disorder than narcissistic personality disorder due to the expected /emotionality' of a woman. Men are more likely, as abusers, to be diagnosed with narcissistic personality disorder because of the power privilege notion, where it is expected for men to act more aggressively and controlling due to their gender. These gender disparities will be discussed more in depth in a later chapter of the book.

Borderline Personality Disorder

Borderline Personality Disorder is a disorder that is so dominant that it falls into the category of personality disorders within the diagnosis of the diagnostic statistical manual (DSM-V). Nine specific symptoms are described within the manual, which was published in 2013 (the most recent version). These symptoms are divided up into five separate categories, or domains, as they are termed within the DSM-V. Of the nine symptoms, a person must express five of them in order to be diagnosed with Borderline Personality Disorder. They are listed as follows:

Domain A: Constant, intense, unstable, and poorly regulated emotional reactions:

1. Affective instability that includes an extreme experience of anger, irritability, anxiety/panic attacks.
2. Anger that is inappropriate contextually and difficult to regulate and control.
3. Constant sensations of emptiness.

Domain B: Behaviors that are impulsive, as well as harmful to the individual and others.

4. Excessive spending, unsafe sexual conduct, substance use, binge eat, reckless driving.
5. Reoccurring suicidal thoughts and behavior, such self-injury (cutting or hitting oneself), usually done when under stress.

This category includes any other behaviors that fall under the category of self-harm or behaviors that cause damage to properties or others.

Domain C: Distorted perceptions of self; high levels of suspiciousness.

6. A constant unstable self-image or sense of self, as well as self-identity.

7. Suspiciousness of others and what they think of you. Paranoid beliefs and constant stress related episodes during the individual feels like the surroundings are unreal.

Other symptoms that could fall under this category are all-or-nothing thinking difficultly lining up thoughts, and an inability to develop rational problem solving skills within social conflicts.

Domain D: The experience of tumultuous and extremely unstable relationships.

8. Going to extreme efforts to avoid real or imagined abandonment.

9. The individual may go back and forth between idealizing a relationship and severely undermining it. These relationships are marked are intensity and instability.

An individual may also have heavily dependent traits and behavior in important relationships. The individual may expect negative behaviors from others, and have difficultly reasoning clearly in stressful social situations.

As an Abuser

There is a similarity between Narcissistic Personality Disorder and Borderline Personality Disorder, which is the constant fear of abandonment. The difference between these two two disorders is the reaction to the real or perceived concepts of that abandonment. A person with borderline personality disorder is more likely to feel reactive because they are capable of some level of empathy and understanding where they perceive a person might leave them. A person with narcissistic personality disorder may interpret this sensation and feel only concern for themselves and how the perceived behavior is making them feel.

It is believing that those with Borderline Personality Disorder have experienced some form of abandonment in their life that greatly stunts their emotional development as well as the ability to appropriately relate to others. It is said that due to their inability to control their anger, they are more likely than the general population to be verbal/emotionally/psychologically abusive.

An article written by AJ Mahari on [18]*Mental Health Matters* describes at length the link between this stunted emotional

---

[18] https://mental-health-matters.com/borderline-personality-and-abuse/

growth and the expression of rage when it comes to abusive behavior:

Intra-Psychic Pain: Siting at the Root

If a person with Borderline Personality Disorder gets close to another, especially in an intimate romantic relationship, instead of experiencing feelings of joy and elation, they experience fear and panic. They are going backwards in their minds to unresolved pain of abandonment that they had previously experienced. This raises maladaptive defenses that the borderline had previously applied in their past experience of pain. The fear, panic and rage rise from the association with this past experience, almost an attempt to 're-do' correctly what they perceived as incorrect in the past. When a borderline person gets close to another, they are simply afraid that due to this closeness, something similar will happen to them that had previously happened in the past.

Borderline Rage

Anger is one of the main emotions experienced by a person with borderline personality disorder. It is believed that this is due to an association with childhood responses, whereas rage acts as a primal feeling generated to protect the self and to entice the caregiver to return back to caring for the infant. It is believed that this is why the anger expressed by a person with borderline personality disorder is so intense, because it precedes cognitive and verbal development.

Anger then becomes associated with survival. If the borderline has achieved closeness in a relationship with a non-borderline, if they exhibit behavior that is not 100% paying keen attention to their partner, this intense rage can be triggered. It can be triggered by something minimal, but the borderline does not have a regulated sense of emotions, and perceives this act as evidence of abandonment, so reverts back to an expression of this rage to help them survive. This rage is always sitting at the surface, which why the experience of it can often be perceived by the partner as surprising and abrupt.

Abuse by the person with borderline personality disorder is expressed differently. Some are very direct, with verbal insults, yelling and screaming, throwing things, whereas others are more passive-aggressive with their rage. Borderlines do not have a gathered sense of self, which is why they can also experience sensations of dissociation. Their experience of past abandonment constantly meshes with experiences of the presently perceived abandonment behaviors.

So then a cycle goes on and on; anything short of intense symbiotic connection that is uninterrupted will cause the borderline to perceive the relationship as going downhill, so the anticipation of the pain occurs as well as the pain associated with the actual abandonment. Abusive behaviors are more likely to occur during the times the combination of rage and vulnerability hit an apex. It repeats itself, as the borderline has no idea what their doing at the time connotes abuse. Some are capable of self-reflection and realize that they have acted poorly. But in general those are not aware of their emotions or how they can behave differently or help themselves in the future. Oftentimes, due to the abuse, the abused actually do leave the borderline, which leads to their worst fears coming into fruition and the likelihood of self-injurious and suicidal behavior.

As the Abused

A study done in 2016 found that emotional abuse was the most significant type of abuse in later diagnosed borderline personality disorder. Those who have experienced sexual and physical abuse who have adult diagnosed borderline personality disorder exist as 40-76% in those who were sexually abused and 25-73% in those who were physically abused. The most studied form of abuse and the link between borderline personality is maltreatment and neglect, whose relationship has been conclusively demonstrated.

Although there is not a lot more conclusive evidence of the link between childhood emotional/psychological abuse and the development of borderline personality, there are several attempts at exploring the symptoms and links behaviorally.[19] Helena Wang wrote an article on the proposed link between childhood abuse and BPD by describing Rejection Sensitivity and Negative Affectivity:

Rejection Sensitivity: This trait vulnerability is high amongst those diagnosed with borderline personality disorder. It is marked as being even higher than those with anxiety disorders. This trait is characterized by an intense expectation of rejection from others, and a higher likelihood to interpret behaviors as rejection by their peers in social interactions. Due to this sensitivity, child will misinterpret ambiguous social interactions as being the favor of rejection, where in reality it is mild or nonexistent. They often find social interactions be more stressful than their peers. Emotions such as frustration, anger, or anxiety expressed by a peer can easily be seen as rejection.

Generally, children with this sensitivity will develop two main coping mechanisms: avoidance and over-attachment. Both are present within the behavioral framework of a persons with borderline personality disorder, and often diagnosed within the

[19] https://wp.nyu.edu/steinhardt-appsych_opus/childhood-emotional-abuse-and-borderline-personality-disorder/

same person. They can simultaneously express these coping mechanisms as they grow order in ways of avoiding social interactions in order to stay away from the possibility of rejection, while also forming intense close relationships with a select few friends. They simply want both a close relationship and fear it at the same time.

Negative Affectivity: This trait is described as possessing a tendency to be easily bothered by emotionally triggering events and feel associated negative emotions in relation to those triggers. This is the trait that is responsible for the intense experience of emotions that the BP experiences. When children with higher negative affectivity are emotionally/psychologically abused their emotional and social growth is hindered, and continue to feel these intense emotions and become easily triggered by other emotions. A child with less negative affectivity will consequently be less likely to have their emotional and social development hindered, and thus, less likely to develop borderline personality disorder.

Thought suppression, a form of therapy applied to treat borderline personality disorder, was once known to significantly decrease the effect of negative affectivity during the development of borderline personality disorder. The practice is when individuals attempt to consciously disassociate themselves from their negative thoughts. It is important to note that this act is overall maladaptive and harmful for the individual practicing it, as well as for anyone with mental health issues. This is because encouraging further disassociations will make it harder to switch the borderline individual back into feeling their emotions and learning to deal with them directly.

Histrionic Personality Disorder

Histrionic Personality disorder is a personality disorder described in the DSM-V. This personality disorder is significantly less known that the other three described in this section, especially when it relates to emotional abuse.

The DSM-V states that for a diagnoses of histrionic personality disorder, five or more of the following listed symptoms must be present:

—Severely self-centered; feels uncomfortable when the attention is not on them.
—Constantly seeks approval and reassurance.
—Often dresses inappropriately in a seductive manner/behaves in an overly inappropriate seductive manner.
—Constantly altering emotional states that appear phony to others.
—Overly obsessive about physical appearance. Uses appearances to draw attention to themselves.

—Opinions are easily influences by others.

—Expresses exaggerated emotions.

—Is highly suggestible.

—Has the tendency to believe that relationships are more intimate than they actually are?

This personality is more commonly diagnosed in women, but it is believed that this is due to the gender disparity previously noted. Attention-seeking and sexual assertiveness are less socially acceptable for women, therefore, when this is present, it is faster to be seen as a behavior of a disorder in women then in men.

Usually people with this personality disorder seek treatment for secondary issues, like when their relationship with their romantic partner ends. They are able to develop depression due to the overly inflated notion of certain relationships in their lives. It is difficult to note when an occurrence is realistic with a person with this disorder because they often exaggerate. They often cannot see a situation in a realistic light. The form of therapy usually applied for those with histrionic personality disorder is psychotherapy due to the commonality of them seeking treatment for their depression. They may break boundaries set by the therapist, and feel emotionally needy toward the therapist.

As the Abuser

Those with histrionic personality disorder are not often identified as abusers because of their emotional sensitivity, a tendency toward depression, the tendency to be overly dramatic and emotional, as well as their sensitivity toward criticism. There has been links in diagnoses of histrionic personality with antisocial personality disorder. Antisocial personality disorder is the disorder that many people often confuse with psychopathy. But once again, in reference to gender disparities, generally men were being diagnosed with anti-social personality. This was more than likely again due to stereotyping the way men and women are expected to behave. 2/3 of individual women who were treated and assessed also met the criteria for antisocial personality disorder.

As the Abused

There is a general link between childhood suffered abuse and the development of personality disorders. Personality disorders are different from other disorders in the sense that they manifest intensely and throughout the entire expression of the person. Anxiety disorders, psychotic disorders, and mood disorders, are focal and generally stay within a couple portions of that individual's life. This allows treatment to be easier for these people, because the disorder is not embedded within their personality. As previously discussed, there are several forms of abuse, and it is in several forms that different personality disorders are more likely to develop. In the case of borderline personality, antisocial, and schizotypal, physical and sexual abuse were mainly associated. Neglect and maltreat, as well as emotional/psychological was mainly liked to borderline personality disorder. There is very little research done on the histrionic personality and its link to abuse, but it has been estimated in general that a histrionic personality along with all the other personality disorders can be linked to some form of childhood trauma.

The Psychopathic Personality

Psychopathy is a disorder related to specific issues with brain functions; a few of the areas that have been studied are the ventromedial prefrontal cortex, amygdala, and the anterior cingulate cortex. Studies over time have indicated a strong genetic foundation within the disorder. It is one of the most deeply ingrained personality disorders that aligns with its own difficultly in being treated. There are approximately (according to Psychology Today), 1-2% of the population ho could be diagnosed with psychopathy, present in both genders. It is a condition that has four specific categories of symptoms, which are as follows: a neurological function, a range of intensity that falls on a spectrum, positive symptoms, and the presence of subtype (either a primary or secondary psychopath).

Here we will highlight some of the most common general symptoms of a person who could be diagnosed with psychopath:

—Lack of or small amount of empathy.
—Intense aggression.
—Strong manipulation skills.
—Arrogance.
—Blame shifting.
—Impulsivity.
—Pathological lying.
—A tendency toward boredom.
—Superficial charm.
—Lack of remorse or guilt.
—Lack of realistic long-term goals.
—Many short term relationships.
—Constant need for stimulation.

There are two categories previously listed that the diagnoses of psychopathy can be placed into: primary and secondary psychopathy.

Primary Psychopathy: These individuals are born with features of higher testosterone and lower active cortisol hormones (the stress hormone). For this kind of psychopathy there is no link between a neurological experience of an emotional and a physical response. This is why it is easy for a psychopath to mimic emotions, body language, and tone of voice in order to simulate empathy.

Secondary Psychopathy: These individuals experience the symptoms of psychopathy due to an occurrence in life that left them traumatized. This could be childhood abuse, neglect, and isolation, and used detachment of emotions in order to avoid feeling results of the trauma or abuse. These individuals are able to come out the other side of the psychopathic process, i.e., respond to treatment. Their psychopathic behavior allows their testosterone to balance out with cortisol, just as it does naturally for the primary psychopath. These individuals possess a genetic predisposition of psychopathy that needs to be triggered in order for the psychopathic behaviors and traits to come to the surface.

As the Abuser

Many of the traits and behaviors of a psychopathic abuser sound very similar to that of a narcissistic abuser. It is important to remember though that there is a clear difference between the two personality disorders; the narcissistic personality genuinely, deep down, requires approval and fears abandonment. The psychopath on the other hand, does not require approval, nor do they fear being abandoned. Some narcissist though can be psychopathic, but not all, as they do express primitive emotions. But most psychopaths do possess narcissistic traits.

Here are the behavior's that are very similar to narcissistic abuse and how they differentiate from psychopathic abuse, according to [20]Psychology today:

1. Pathological Lying/Manipulation: The desire for power in a relationship is stronger than the desire for connection for a psychopath. It has been said that lying, for psychopaths, is a lot like breathing. It is that simple and easy. They will literally make up anything in order to achieve their goals. Lies, deceptions, victim blaming, all fall under this category of psychopathic abuse. They repeated them consistently to distort the perspective of the person they are in a relationship with.

2. Morality Lacking and Breaking Rules: Psychopaths have either very little or no sense of morality. Most of the population are born and grow up understanding the basic concepts of right and wrong in simple terms; hitting another person is wrong, being polite is right, etc. This is not the case for psychopaths. All behavior exists on single continuum, and if it benefits them, then it doesn't matter what the action may be. They often live under the motto that rules are meant to be broken. If morality

---

[20] https://www.psychologytoday.com/ca/blog/communication-success/201810/7-characterisitics-the-modern-psychopath

is ever expressed, then it is being used as a tool to further a hidden agenda. In a romantic relationship, morality can be easily faked, in order to feign empathy should the partner believe their partner is not acting correctly.

3. Lack of Empathy: The previous issues mentioned about the prefrontal cortex, which is the most advanced region of the brain, connect to this section. This is the area that is responsible for regulated the capacity to understand other people's feelings, and the ability to make judgment calls, as well as the capacity to learn from life experiences. The issues with the prefrontal cortex with psychopaths means that they lack all of these functions. Abuse then, is a lot easier to commit, because they are not bothered by guilt, which is an emotion spurred on by empathy. Emotional/psychological abuse is committed without second thought so they can get what they want, or so the partner can behave the way that they specifically desire.

4. Narcissism: As previously mentioned, the majority of psychopaths possess narcissistic personality traits. The connection to abuse and narcissistic personality disorder with psychopathy is the belief of inferiority, which allows the individual mistreat others to their benefit.

5. Gas lighting: This tactic was previously discussed in the section that spoke about the narcissistic abuser. This is a category of behaviors that serves to confuse the partner into believing falsehoods, or to convince the partner that they event did not

occur. Gas lighting allows the psychopath to manipulate their partner into believing lies about themselves, their stupidity, unattractiveness, lack of friends, etc.

6. Lack of Remorse and Self-Serving Victimhood: Not showing remorse in a relationship does not further along the intimacy of that relationship. When a psychopathic person is caught in the act of horrific behavior and abuse, they express their lack of remorse through blaming the victim-blaming and increasing the consistency of their aggressive behavior. If they can play themselves are the victim and it furthers their story, they then will do it

As the Abused

There is a higher prevalence of child abuse occurring and the association of developing psychopathy. Findings in a study conducted in Italy in 2003 found that early exposure to relational trauma were found among participants who obtained high scores on the psychopathic scale. Another study found that even witnessing domestic violence within a household can result in psychopathic traits as they grow older. The study, of course, is not a guarantee that experiencing abuse directly causes psychopathic traits. There is somewhat of an association between the manipulative and negative behaviors of the abusive parents, and then grow up to mimic similar behaviors. It is also possible that children learn to manipulate and lie in order to avoid becoming victims, or further victims of abuse.

Information associated with abuse and the development of psychopathic traits are still highly scant. But there is still some association.

Here are some ways that different forms of abuse can possibly encourage the existence of psychopathic traits later on in life:

—Children placed in multiple foster homes, adoption programs, or residential treatment centers have the higher likelihood of having stunted emotional growth and less empathy due to the experience of consistent trauma.
—Not forming attachments early on in life due to consistent abuse makes the children in constant survival mode, and in order to survive, they must not form attachments.
—Not attaching leads to the protection of their emotions. They will not get hurt or feel as if they are being abandoned if they do not attach to anyone.
—If these issues are not faced early on in life, the child often grows up into a teenager that commits crimes with conduct disorder, and then possibly grows into an adult with psychopathic traits.

A study conducted at the Norwegian University of Science and technology interviewed prisoners in a high-security facility and found that there are two-forms of parenting styles that can be associated with developing psychopathic traits: total parent neglect and rigidly controlling parenting.

More than half of the psychopaths studied reported that they had been exposed to parenting that falls on the extreme scale of care, either neglectful or extreme control. Most parenting styles fall within the middle of this opposing spectrum. The extreme actions of trying to control a child or completely neglecting them leads in estimation to behavior that is also extreme in order to act out against the abusive actions of the individual's parents.

Conduct disorder is a disorder that usually precedes psychopathy, and is diagnosed within childhood and adolescence. There are two possible course of development that are currently believed to lead to conduct disorder. The first one is called the 'childhood-onset type." This occurs when the symptoms of conduct disorder are present before the age of ten years old. This is linked to more pervasive behaviors that cover the entire personality of the child. They usually have neuropsychological deficits, academic problems, family abuse and higher levels of aggression and violence. The second course is known as the 'adolescent-onset type'. This occurs when the conduct disorder symptoms are present after the age of ten years old. These individuals show less impairment in association with their disorder due to it arriving later in life.

The term psychopathy is a thrown around term that is usually associated with serial killers, rapists, and those who are consistently violent. In relation to this book, it is important to note that not all psychopaths are violent or commit crimes. Many of them are CEO's, leaders in some capacity, surgeons, police officers, etc. And they can function without committing any form of physical violence. They use their skills of manipulation, superficial charm, and pathological lying in order to emotionally/psychologically abuse a partner, a child, an elderly individual. Everything is about personal gain, and morality and emotion are easily simulated. These individuals commit abuse in an emotional/psychological way without applying violence because of their psychopathic nature. Psychopaths do abuse in physical and sexual ways as well. The narcissistic personality is also capable of committing physical and sexual abuse. The differences described in this section of the book may help you in identifying the traits that exist within the person you believe is abusing you, a friend, a coworker, etc. Both the psychopath and the narcissistic personality are incredibly capable of applying abuse that connotes emotional/psychological abuse. It may be less relevant to identify the category of a person's disorder who is committing the abuse than to take note of their behavior and how it is negatively effecting you, or your friend, or coworker.

The next section will focus on the inward traits of you that may contribute to why you are drawn to the individual of whom who is abusing you. Identifying these traits is not an act that is meant to give the responsibility of the abuse to you, the abused. There is no occasion when any kind of abuse is being committed that it will ever be the responsibility of the abused. There are natural traits developed in childhood that may have given you a predisposition to be attracted to individuals such as narcissists and/or psychopaths.

Falling for Them again: The Codependent Relationship

Codependency is defined as an excessive emotional and psychological reliance on a person, one of whom usually has a mental health, physical health issue, or substance abuse disorder. A code pendent romantic relationship is when a person derives confidence and self-esteem from taking care of their partner, who may seem to be in constant crisis.

Narcissists and Codependents

"Why don't we go? For any combination of reasons. Take a look at the 'you' before or at the time you started going out with the N - and the 'you' later on. Never was anyone less equipped to get out by that stage - your self worth Is in the gutter, you feel a failure, a deep sense of being a nothing - the things the N said to you, the Insidious drip-feed of negatives, their behavior that says so much about how little they respect or care for you. Then of course we really do have to face some of the nastiest - the what Ifs, the depression, the self-hatred (how COULD I have put up with this, how DARE he did this to me without a blink of the eye - what must he have thought of me knowing I allowed him to do these things), the loneliness, sense of failure."

As previously described, narcissists are individuals who are only aware of their own inner world; their emotions, their thoughts, their experiences, their memories. The concept of empathy is an empty void within their emotional capability, so relaying a narcissist how you feel is a waste of time, no matter how detailed your description may be. On the other hand, a person who with a codependent personality is the opposite—the feel deep empathy, and pride themselves on 'fixing' or 'saving' other people. Therefore, relationships between narcissist and codependents often thrive based on their opposing traits that continuously feed upon one other's subconscious needs. An emotionally/psychologically abusive narcissist requires constant support and praise about their abilities due to their deep-seated fear of rejection, so the codependent feeds this need because they function and value themselves through helping others.

If your interpretation as to whether or not you or a friend who is being abused may possess these personality traits, take a read over these six identifying traits of a codependent individual, written by Shawn M. Burn from [21]*Psychology Today*:

1. You have an unearthly pattern of being responsible for others behavior and to want to save them from their issues.
2. Your self-esteem gets boosted by the concept of self-sacrificing yourself for others.
3. You stay in detrimental care taking relationships despite the negative toll on you and your relationships.
4. You consistently try to take care of troubled people whose issues are much larger than what you can handle alone.
5. You attract people who are seeking someone to take care of them.
6. You have a pattern of engaging with well-intentioned behavior in order to help others but it constantly becomes unhealthy for you.

Codependents generally have a difficulty time realizing that they attract narcissists in their lives, or that a parent or partner into he past may have begin this pattern of behavior. The complimentary nature of codependents and narcissist makes it harder to identify and recognize when the relationship is unhealthy and toxic.

---

[21] https://www.psychologytoday.com/us/blog/presence-mind/201604/six-hallmarks-codependence

Everything flows perfectly, seemingly at least, so why would anyone want to stop it?

It takes a long time for codependents to identify what is occurring to them as abuse, because they believe so strongly in the power of their dedication; they mistake self-sacrifice and giving for love. This can happen when a child takes care of a parent with an addiction, or a person believes they are taking care of their partner when they are being emotionally abusive. The codependent views them as needing to be saved, so they do, over and over again, waiting for the chance to receive an equal amount of dedication in return. This of course never comes, because all the narcissist requires is to be taken care of and constantly reassured.

Codependent believe that they are only valuable through their actions; what they give, rather than being wanted as partner/child/friend for the positive qualities possess. Their low self-esteem allows them to believe that no one would love them for who they truly are, so they continue this constant giving toward their narcissistic partner. The partner, or parent, continues to thrive, because through the systematically emotional/psychological abuse, they are able to utilize the useful tool on their sensitive codependent. Guilt, name-calling, belittling, are all useful tools in the narcissist toolbox, because it keeps the codependent in place, maintains low self-esteem, and maintains the flow of care taking without reciprocation.

If you feel that you identify as a codependent, please read over the list written above a few more times. It is not uncommon for people to return back to their abusers, whether it be in a relationship or familial relation. It takes time to realize that your relationship is unhealthy and not a positive influence in your life. When this occurs in romantic relationships, especially long-term ones, it is normal for the abused/codependent to feel as if they could never find anyone in their lives that would treat them better.

This book is here to tell you that that statement is untrue. It is more than possible for you to self-reflect and learn to identify behaviors and tendencies that led you back to engaging with narcisistici people. It is very possible to rebuild your sense of self-esteem and confidence that the narcissist managed to pull down your entire life.

Halting the Cycle: What to Do

The first step is to identify the cycle of abuse, and to follow through on identifying your own codependent tendencies. Here, both will be reiterated as was previous stated in other chapters. When a child or elderly person is being abused, it is harder for them to notice the cycle of abuse and actually put a halt to it themselves. Therefore, this section is relevant to those who may be around a person of whom they are suspecting is being emotionally/psychologically abused.

In Domestic Relationships

As previously stated, the general cycle of abuse flows as such: tension building, incident, reconciliation, and calm. In a romantic relationship, it is more than likely most common to identify an emotionally/psychologically abusive situation during the incident and reconciliation situation. An article written about domestic violence/abuse from [22]*Help Guide* identifies questions one can ask about themselves or their partner:

Ask Yourself:
—Do you feel afraid of your partner?
—Do you avoid topics out of fear of angering them?
—Do you believe you deserve to be hurt or not treated well?
—Do you wonder about your own sanity?
—Do you feel numb or helpfulness?
—Does your partner humiliate you often?
—Does your partner blame you for their own abusive behavior?

---

[22] https://www.helpguide.org/articles/abuse/domestic-violence-and-abuse.htm/

—Does your partner put you down for your accomplishments?

—Does your partner see you as an object rather than a person?

—Does your partner force you into sexual intercourse?

—Does your partner threaten you with violence?

—Does your partner threaten suicide?

—Does your partner keep you from seeing friends or family?

—Does your partner constantly check up on you?

—Does your partner have an unpredictable temper?

If the answer to most of these questions is yes, then it is likely that you are in an emotionally abusive relationship. Realizing this, is very important. The very first step in **recognizing** that the behavior your partner is committing is abuse.

The next step is **realizing that it is not your fault.** There is never any circumstance in an abusive situation where the fault lies on the abused. This is a fallacy that the abuser attempts to convinces their victim over a long period of cyclic behaviors. This is a huge step, and usually don't a fair amount of effort through the support of loved ones. This must occur by no longer making any excuses for the abuse; no matter how unintelligent, unreliable, or undesirable you believe you are, there is no excuse for behavior that is abusive. The abuser wants you to think that no one else will be able to love you like they do, therefore, you do not think leaving is possible or practical. This is the key to the narcissist's malevolent tactics.

Once it is recognized that you are being abused, and you are convinced that it is not your fault, it is time **to begin documenting** everything. Now the concept of leaving is realistic and possible. This is very important if you have children or are married. Journal entries are a tactic, or even audio/visual recordings if possible are good ideas should it be available. If the abuse is physical, attaining a restraining order would be very important too. Keep the documents in a safe place that your partner cannot locate, or even at someone's house that you trust.

Packing an emergency bag is very important. This too can have kept at a person's house in whom you trust. Keep anything that is essential to a couple days or even a week of functioning, such as medication, identification, and money. Abusive situations can escalate very quickly, and you have to be ready to leave at a moment's notice.

Alerting your family and friends is a good decision once you or someone who is being abused is able to admit that they are in an abusive situation. Support of people you love and who love you are going to be highly important during this difficult time. The abuser may have been masterful at separating you from those you love in order to avoid support of leaving. Once you realize you are being abused, trying to reach out to family and friends again is something that may be difficult, especially if the abuser was successful in keeping you separated. But stay dedicated, and realize that the separation created is another tactic your abuser applies.

Finally, the act of **leaving and completely disengaging** from this partner is the most crucial activity to participate in to begin the process of healing. The act of leaving is both physical and mental. An abuser can react to this separation with unkind acts, or flowers, in an attempt to continue the cycle of abuse. It is important to realize that these behaviors are them trying to bring you back, and keep you controlled. Make the effort to block the abuser on social media, email, and phone number, along with your restraining order. Remind yourself that this person injured you, whether it be physically or emotionally. This person is not going to stop their behavior. You cannot love them out of their abuse. The only way it will stop is for you to actually leave the situation, and begin identifying your own tendencies toward codependent behavior.

With Children and the Elderly

The act of halting the cycle of abuse with children and elderly is harder to recognize due to it being a second party. A teacher may notice the lack of development of a child if they are being emotionally/abused, and the abrupt occurrence of depression and anxiety in an older person noticed by a caretaker. Initially, especially with children, it is going to be more difficult to change the cycle of abuse, especially if you are not directly related to the child. The easiest way to identify emotional/psychological abuse of a child is through the infliction of other forms of abuse, mostly neglect. If a child is unwashed, often hungry or comes to school without a lunch or snack, appears underdeveloped, etc., it way be easier to identify further emotional/psychological abuse if it is occurring at home. Of course if this kind of abuse is being committed upon a child by a caretaker, such as a teacher or babysitter, abuse can be directly cut off by halting care or reporting the person. This is the same for an elderly individual who is being cared for in a retirement home.

Identifying Your Own Codependent Tendencies

"After about a month no contact, he was back on bended knees begging to 'negotiate his surrender' to me. He asked me to marry him. I fell for it again and the drinking started again. Shortly after the wedding, the fighting started again. I realized that drinking was lowering my inhibitions and I let out all of the anger I was still carrying from the prior devaluation. Then I discovered all his lies regarding his business, which he considered 'his little secret'. After

6 months of marriage he came home from a business trip, waited 'til the next morning after I left for work and moved out."

In domestic relationships, once you have managed to disengage from your abusive partner, there will come a time during the healing process that you must reflect upon yourself and identify your own codependent traits. Whether or not years down the road you would like to date again, there is an extreme likelihood that if you were exhibiting codependent tendencies in a romantic relationship then you have exhibiting them in others. With parents, friends, it is important to notice these tendencies so you do not fall into another pattern of codependency in your life.

Codependency in romantic relationships isn't entirely unhealthy within itself. There is always a level of it involved, it is only when it becomes one-sided and toxic, such as the patterns of narcissist and codependent, that it becomes unhealthy.

Previously questions were posed about you and your relationship with your partner. Now, try asking these questions about yourself as you go through your own relationship history with honesty and compassion (posed by Beth Gilbert of [23]*Everyday Health*):

—Do you have difficulty making decisions in a relationship?
—Do you have difficulty identifying your feelings?
—Do you lack trust in yourself?
—Do you have low self-esteem?

[23] https://www.everydayhealth.com/emotional-health/do-you-have-a-codependent-personality.aspx

—Do you have fears of abandonment?

—Do you have obsessive needs for approval?

—Do you have an exaggerated responsibility for the actions of others?

Try writing these questions down, and their answers. Give yourself examples that you can look back on directly. Remember that codependency is a learned behavior, so you can unlearn it as well. Here are some steps that you can take to help yourself heal from your abusive relationship and to notice when you are falling back into patterns of codependency:

—Do your best to be honest with yourself and others? This includes the person of whom you may believe you are being codependent upon after you have disengaged from the abusive relationship. Even when your partner tries to lure you back in, be honest in recognizing that they are trying to use your codependent tendencies against you.

—Be mindful of negative thoughts. Try to notice when you start to think that you deserve to be treated badly, put a halt to it and remember that it simply is not true, and replace them but positive thoughts. Research Cognitive Behavioral Therapy (CBT) to find exercises that can help you build up this pattern of thinking.

—Work on not taking things personally. It is difficult for a codependent person not to take the behavior of others as a direct negative act meant to harm them. Negative actions of others are not your responsibility, nor is it your responsibility to fix their flaws.

—Try to take breaks from people of whom you believe you are in a codependent relationship with. Once you have left the abusive relationship, you may start noticing that you are codependent upon your parents, friends, or even siblings. It is healthy every now and then to take time to yourself and understand what makes you relaxed and happy, as opposed to focusing all your energy upon other person.

—Consider counselling and peer support. Once you have disengaged from your partner it is difficult to keep up the patterns of not thinking negatively, not taking things personally, and maintaining an honest relationship with yourself. Sharing with others who have had similar experiences can help the healing process immensely. Co-dependents anonymous is a 12-step program created to emulate the program Alcoholics Anonymous that can help people share their experiences of being codependent.

—Establish clear boundaries. People with codependent personalities have trouble identifying where their needs and others lie in the universe separately. Setting boundaries helps you realize when you are crossing the line and sinking back into codependent behaviors.

Most people who feel they have codependent personalities say that they do not know the differences between their codependent behaviors and what it means to love. If this is how you feel, know that you are not alone, and are greatly capable of change.

Power Privilege and Personality

Power privilege refers to the use of power from a position that is exempt from prosecutions that others must face as a result of the same behavior. In the context of abuse, it is most common for men to above their power privilege in heterosexual relationships and toward their female inferiors in an authoritative position. The link between genders and narcissist tendencies was found in a study conducted in 2015, one that spanned over 31 years and exposed men as exemplifying these traits more than women of all ages. Men in leadership positions were more likely to be assertive and desire to exert power over others. The behavior of men in abusive relationships shows that their controlling nature means they feel entitled toward this control, which connects to the misuse of power. This power privilege is directly coordinated with the narcissistic personality to form an overall abusive individual.

It is mainly men who form this blend in personality when it comes to domestically abusive relationships, but women can as well. Narcissism is a trait that can carry over genders, orientations, and cultures, especially when it comes to the abuse of children and the elderly.

Chapter 4: The Narcissist, and the Difference Between Male and Female Abusers

All forms of emotional/psychological abuse can be committed by a person of any gender they may identify with. In heterosexual relationships, it was once thought that women who abuse men were not that common. It turns out that is more common then previously imagined, with much of the shame being derived from toxic societal beliefs of what it means to be male and the concept of masculinity. The following chapter will focus on the differences between male and female's abusers where it relates to the elderly, children, and domestic relationships. This chapter will mainly focus on the differences in intimate partner relationships and abuse.

Emotional/Psychological Abuse Committed by a Male

When its a Parent

In an article written on [24]*Psychology Today*, Susanne Babble describes the story of Dianna, a young girl who grew up in the

---

[24] https://www.psychologytoday.com/ca/blog/somatic-psychology/201205/escape-emotionally-and-verbally-abusive-father

Middle East and was emotionally/psychologically abused by her Father. Her story describes noticing when she felt like her mother was being mistreated, and standing up for her as she got older. She notes a man who was controlling, demeaning, and treated her mother like a person who was not equal, as opposed to his wife. The intense lack of respect is something that she noticed from a very early age.

It is common for children to notice this kind of behavior being committed upon their mother as they begin to grow up. Usually when a child is emotionally/psychologically abused by a parent, the opposing parent is being abused as well. This was the same in Dianna's story, as she began noticing his behavior transfer over to her as she got older. She noted times when he would yell at her for hours on end; telling her she wasn't doing good enough at school, not being good enough to him, not doing anything right around the house. She confessed how low she felt, and yet, how confused she would be when days later would be the kindest person, spoiling her and adoring her.

This is a clear display of the cycle of abuse; the blowup, and then the cool down. Dianna did not realize she was being emotionally/psychologically abused until her mother read Patricia Evan's book *The Verbally Abusive Relationship: How to Recognize It and to Respond*. From her perspective as child, she always believed that her Father was right simply because he was her father.

Dianna's Fathers abuse took a toll on her as a child, and maintained a hold on her as she grew up. When she attended college, he expected her to answer her phone every time he called. His yelling and name-calling made her brain foggy. She fell into a depression when she felt like she was not doing well in school, which furthered the consistency of her Father's abuse. Once her mother and her were able to finally leave the abusive situation, they both continued to suffer from post-traumatic stress, depression, and anxiety. Dianna's Father was extremely well-liked in her community and friends, therefore, made it harder for other's believe the intensity of his abuse.

Many children though grow up without knowing that their Father or parent was emotionally/psychologically abusive toward them. It may only be through their own behaviors, mental health issues, or tendency toward abuse that they are able to look back and in hindsight see that their parent's actions were not healthy. [25]*The Mighty* asked readers about their behaviors that they did not realize they were committed due to the emotionally/psychologically abusive actions of their Fathers as children:

---

[25] https://themighty.com/2018/03/abusive-father-affected-my-mental-health/

108

—Invalidating of emotions occurs when a person feels that what they feel is wrong, and believe that they have 'no right to be upset.' Victims often feel like they don't know how to express their emotions constructively.

—Females noted that they may attach themselves to any man who treats them even slightly better than their Fathers.

—Heterosexual females do not believe their male partners when they are being validated or appreciated.

—The inability to be around people having an argument. Feeling on edge and on the verge of tears when voices escalate to yelling.

—Constant self blame.

—Females avoiding men at all costs.

—The expectation to be put down or insulted.

—Constant apologies for things that are not one's responsibility.

—A sensitivity toward loud sounds, quick gestures.

—Avoiding learning to do new things because the assumption is that they are going to fail.

When its a Partner

While it is believed that 75% of narcissists are men, there is a possibility that when observing disordered traits that the symptoms are mistakenly gendered. Women can be more so diagnosed as Borderline Personality or Histrionic Personalities, but this does not mean that they do not express narcissistic tendencies. The majority of this book has focused on the behaviors of the male narcissist, because it is the most common. Here will be listed the most behavioral traits of a male narcissistic abuser. These will generally occur because of the previously discussed power privilege that men in most societies feel over women in heterosexual relationships, but also in same sex ones:

—Mind Games: Some mind games such as gaslighting are applied in order to display power of the partner and their seeming superior intelligence. When the victim is a woman, it may be believed that men are the superior gender, and allow doubt about her own realities to cross her mind due to previously existing sensations of inferiority.

—Control over Finances: In heterosexual relationships, if men are the primary breadwinners then they will use their position to treat women like a child in relation to finances. They may keep information regarding money from them, and force them to ask permission to spent it. They also use this as a tactic to obsessively stalk when their partner may be up to when they are not around.

—Accusation of affairs: If the victim is a codependent, then it is easy for them to believe that they constantly need to make their partner feel validated. If a male partner accuses their female partner of flirting or having an affair, they force their partner into the position of 'proving' their dedication and love to them. This can show its face in the form of forcing sexual activities, or to 'consent' to allowing them to be track financially, or report to their partner what they are doing at all times.

—Using the children: There are many ways that a male can use children as weapons in an emotionally/psychologically abusive relationship. First of all, he can have undermined her abilities and use them as further examples as to why she is not a competent person. A lot of women, especially if they are already codependent, attach a great amount of their identity within their perceived performance as a parent. Taking care of the child is a part of their codependent natures. If that is criticized, then they can feel greatly emotionally injured. Secondly, if a woman is attempting to leave a man due to his emotional/psychological abuse toward her, it is likely that he will threaten gaining custody over the children and further criticize her for 'tearing the family apart.' Children are easy points of reference when it comes to finding something that will make a women feel instantly vulnerable.

—Criticism of appearance: A lot of women place importance on their appearance due to societal stereotypes and incorrect assumptions. Some women, especially if they are being emotionally /psychologically abused, believe that they must maintain an overall perceived 'attractive' appearance at all times. A man can easily criticize how a woman looks, her weight, her perceived desirableness in order to maintain the notion that no one else is going to want them the way their partner does. Even if he criticizes her constantly, to the abused, they may be doing them a 'favor' by pointing out what is wrong with them.

According to *Spring Tide Resources*, 35% of all women who are or have been married or common-law have experienced emotional abuse. [26]A study conducted by the same website stated 72% of women reported that emotional abuse was responsible for feelings of depression and anxiety. The greatest impact on them was ridicule, jealousy, and isolation. Women who are emotionally/psychologically abused are also more likely to suffer from physical abuse by their male partners.

[26] https://www.springtideresources.org/resource/emotional-abuse-women-male-partners-facts

Being female, according to the [27]*American Psychological Association* and a thorough study titled *Violence and the Family*, is the single largest risk factor for being a victim of abuse in a heterosexual relationship. This clearly shows the placement that women have in society as existing as an inferior being.

Emotional/Psychological Abuse Committed by a Female

"She actually never had emotions for me nor does she harbor guilt over what she's done. I mean, I just can't fathom that. She said so many beautiful things to me! The reality that all that may have been a crock, Is overwhelmingly Inconceivable."

When it is a Parent

Females are able to emotionally/psychologically abuse their children as much as men are. Whereas it used to be seen as acting strict when a male would excuse their behavior as 'discipline' the identical actions of a mother connote different effects. Females in heterosexual relationships as the mother are stereotypically seen as the more 'loving' or 'nurturing' one due to societal expectations. Therefore, when a mother emotionally/psychologically abuses their child, there is a distinct

---

[27] American Psychological Association, *Violence and the Family*, Report of the American Psychological Association Presidential Task Force on Violence and the Family, 1996:19.

confusion that occurs within the minds and lives of both their male or female's children.

[28]*The Mighty* also asked adults about the effects of mothers who emotionally/psychologically abused them as children. Some results that differ from that of Father's who abuse were as follows:

—Having difficulty receiving gifts or compliments because the association with them is negative. The victim may still believe that they do not deserve this praise, or that there are strings attached toward receiving the gift.

—Constantly worry about what other people think of you.

—Obsessively fearing abandonment. The victims don't feel good enough to be loved, therefore, they assume that anyone who claims to care about them is going to leave them at a moments notice.

—Changing the subject when talking about moms. A lot of victims shut down when other people talk about their positive relationship with their mom due to their abusive past.

---

[28] https://themighty.com/2018/01/growing-up-narcissistic-emotionally-abusive-mother/

—Putting other people's needs before their own. This is the desire to constantly please others that is implementing during emotional/psychologically abuse. It also happens to avoid confrontation and abandonment.

—Working toward perfection. Due to constant criticism from their mothers as children, or even continuing as adults, victims feel the need to never make mistakes and to make sure everything they do is perfect. They often excessively berate themselves for days after making a mistake, no matter how small others may believe the mistake may be.

—Avoidance of physical intimacy.

—Craving physical intimacy also occurs. The victim may want to do their best to avoid becoming their mother, who may have not physically expressed their affection toward them.

—Questioning if you are a good parent. Comparing yourself to the behavior of your mother occurs because of the jealousy some women may feel when they hear about the positive relationships some of their friends may have with their mothers.

—Wishing for the mother you never had. Many victims may attach themselves to mother figures, such as a friend's mother, or individuals in the media. This can also be expressed through the various codependent tendencies previously expressed, such as the desire to fix others, even though you are aware that it is not your responsibility.

—Always trying to live up to your mother's standards occurs because it is difficult to disengage from an emotionally/psychologically abusive relationship in general. Confusing love and codependency happens too when mothers continue their cycle of abuse into adulthood, leading to more occurrences of resentment.

When it is a Partner

It was once believed that women do not commit abuse toward their male partners due to the false concept of superiority of men in society. It is only recently being discovered that due to shame and this false sense of toxic masculinity that a lot of men do not disclose abuse, or even have a difficult time reporting it due to their self-belief. A study conducted by Human Services looked at abuse committed by women onto men between 1999 and 2004, and found that six percent of men in intimate relationships have experienced abuse or violence from their partners.

The motivation behind females committing abuse upon their male or same sex partners is the same as males committing it, which is the desire for power and control. A lot of the same tactics are utilized, such as belittling, gaslighting, and threatening, but there are also some that are unique because it is a woman committing the abuse in the relationship.

Due to society's attitudes toward men and the belief that due to this physical strength as male that they cannot be abused, they may not be taken seriously. Here are some feelings, listed by Human Services, that a man may be feeling when his female partner is emotionally/psychologically abusive:

—Possesses a fear of telling anyone about the abuse.
—Feels humiliated.
—Feels depressed.
—Feels as if he has failed as a partner or 'man.'
—Confused because sometimes the partner is loving.
—He fear losing his identity as a man if it is found out what is occurring.
—He may feel guilty about leaving her to cope alone.
—He may feel frustrated because he has tried everything to make it work.
—He may believe he deserves it.

Not every person who abuses is the victim of abuse themselves, but women who were victims of abuse themselves have a higher likelihood of either becoming an abuse victim again, or to become an abuser themselves. Kimberly Taylor, author of *Exposing the Abusive Female,* interviewed women who were the sole abusing in a heterosexual relationship. She found that these women were more likely to apply nonphysical tactics, like emotional/psychological abuse onto their partners than physical violence. Here are some common traits that she noted about these women who abused their partners:

—Manipulation and controlling tactics.
—Using the children against their partner, such as threatening to take the children away.
—Possessive behavior.
—Expressing extreme jealousy.
—High impulsivity.
—Extreme anger and rage.
—Not having enough outside support from other female friends.
—Apply name calling that emasculates their partner.

The reason why men are fuelled by shame and are more likely to hide abuse from their partners is due the mistaken beliefs as to what what connotes a man as a male. Listed here are some stereotypical notions and deeply rooted notions that make a lot of men hide away and suffer abuse in silence:

—That men are more physical, stronger, and 'should' be able to handle an abusive partner.

—That men always want sex, therefore, should never complain that their partner is sexually abusing them.

—That being emotional is a chiefly female trait.

—That men who express vulnerability is 'weak'.

—That the expression of anger and aggression are what make them masculine.

—That the exertion of power over their partner is how t hey can express their masculinity in relationships.

Oddly enough, the above list is also false beliefs that allow abusive men to continue behaving the way they do toward female victims. As society progresses, it is important to realize that abusers are of all genders and orientations, and that there needs to exist programs that can help victims; no matter their gender or orientation.

Chapter: 5 Recovering from Emotional and Narcissistic Abuse

"The hardest thing Is saying to yourself: 'I cannot go back THERE ... so I must move forward'. Maybe It was familiarity that kept us there ... but fear Is my biggest hang-up. Fear of the unknown! I guess we traded a few moments of happiness with them when actually It was hell on earth!"

Finally, you have managed to disengage from your narcissistic abuser. You have begun identifying traits that may make you more vulnerable toward falling under your ex-partner or parents' spell, and are working at it daily. But what else can you do to help yourself or those you those recover from emotional and narcissistic abuse? This chapter will site some suggestions, and explain why you or someone you know may not be ready to start the change they need in order to live a healthy and fulfilling life.

Change Begins with You

Statistics can be listed, advice given, support expressed, but at the end of the day it always comes down to the person being abused who needs to make the decision in order to leave their partner. Educating oneself through books and the understanding of the cycle of abuse is one important way to become aware of abuse, but there are also stages that a person must go through before they are able to stand up and fight for themselves. These are called the stages of change.

Using the Stages of Change to Help Domestic Abuse Victims

The Transtheoretical Model stages of change was written in the 1970s initially to track individuals who were having difficulty quitting smoking. Since then the five stages have been listed in relation to substance abuse, and the processes involved that one must go through in order to recover from addiction. More recently, the stages have been associated with all forms of change in a person's life. Now, these stages of change can be related to people who are trying to recover from intimate partner abuse.

[29]In 2001 a study was conducted at the University of North Carolina that followed the counselling and treatment of individuals who were victims of abuse and how they processed through the various stages of change. That study will be summarized here through the description of the stages, common behaviors, and how those who have already been through the stages managed to maintain complete disengagement for the rest of their lives.

---

[29] https://ocfp.on.ca/docs/cme/using-the-stages-of-change-model-to-counsel-victims-of-intimate-partner-violence.pdf

1. Pre-contemplation: When victims are not aware of, or minimize the problem at hand. This can reveal itself through denial, expressed hopelessness, and resistance toward the physician's inquiries or suggestions of abuse. Some victims may actually admit abuse at some point, but will quickly rationalize the behavior in reference to a particular occurrence. This is called minimization. At this point the victim does not want to change, nor are they seeking help in order to get out of the abusive situation; usually, they are seeking help because of a secondary issue that friends and family may have noticed; such as insomnia, anxiety, or depression.

2. Contemplation: When the problem is acknowledging and changes are considered. This is when the abused become aware that the behavior their partner is exhibiting is not appropriate. The victim may acknowledge the abuse to a close friend. Victims at this stage usually have indefinite plans to escape their partner's behavior, but appears more imaginary than tangible. Victims are struggling to face the reality of their situation at this point. Counsellors may ask a question such as 'why can't you leave?' This is done in order to identify barriers and consequences to the departure. This stage may last a long time till the next stage occurs. But it is believed that it is during this stage that the abused begin to imagine a possible future where the abuse does not exist.

3. Preparation: This is where plan making happens. A person in this situation has acknowledge that there is a problem, and are participating in behavior that will lead them up to actually taking action and leaving their abuser. They begin seeking practical assistance such as financial security, documents like birth certificate, and safe relocation of children if they are present in the relationship. A carefully constructed plan is more likely to succeed through the action and maintenance stage. Counsellors and physicians continue to encourage change and steps that aid them in preparation, but only the victim can decide when they choose to take action.

4. Action: Finally, the victim takes action toward which they have prepared. There is a high level of activity and commitment during this stage. A victim may begin attending a support group, ask their partner for a divorce, depart from their current job in order to achieve financial security, etc. Advocates and those who support the victim have noted in other studies that a victim may make seven to eight attempts to leave, then return to their partner, before they actually leave for good. The return to the abuser can be likened to relapse for a person suffering addiction; it is expected, and highly common. When this occurs, it is not a failure of the victim, or of those who are supporting them.

5. Maintenance : This occurs when the victim has successfully left their abusive partner, but continue to suffer from problem behavior that leads them back to them. The success is often

highly dependent upon the thoroughness of the action plan and the amount of support's the victim is receiving. Counsellors connecting them to other supports before the action and maintenance stage will help the victim be more successful throughout.

The Truth Will Set You free

"At the time I thought I'd never be strong again, but in retrospect I would have to say it as better to have loved and LEARNED than to have not loved at all. Because now I know, beyond a shadow of a doubt, that I will never allow anyone to treat me that way again."

One of the hardest steps to make in order to escape an emotionally/psychologically abusive relationship is realizing that you are being abused. It is usually secondary behaviors that lead people to seek help, and through the exploration of these symptoms, lead them to realize that what they are enduring is not healthy. You, or the person you are supporting, genuinely believes that they are not a worthwhile person, and that their partner's estimation in them being worthless is an actual fact. So why would they, or you, seek help for something that they perceive to be the truth?

If you are questioning as to whether or not you are being emotionally abused, think about how you and your partner interact. Think about how they speak to you, the words they use with you, and think about whether or not you would speak to a child that way. Then think about how often this occurs in your relationship. Try to think about what you felt about yourself when you weren't in a relationship. Realize now, that no matter how down you might feel about yourself, no person has the right to talk down to you and make you feel worthless, unattractive, untalented, or unwanted. You deserve to love and be loved with respect.

Maintaining Dignity with Boundaries

Once you have disengaged completely from your abusive partner, the maintenance stage involves setting healthy boundaries that will keep you from participating in problem behaviors. This should be committed upon while seeking healing through counselling and identifying your own codependent behaviors.

Here are five different ways that you can start setting boundaries for yourself to begin this new, enjoyable and balanced stage of your life, listed by [30]Melaney Oliver on her website. These boundaries can help you out in other relationships too, and prevent you from being taken advantage of:

---

[30] https://melany-oliver.com/5-ways-to-start-setting-boundaries-after-emotional-abuse/

1. Re-examining your Values: Taking a look at your values will help you treat yourself better. You will look at your behavior and thought patterns differently, and will try to focus in on one that align more with your point of view. They can change throughout a lifetime, which is normal. But now is the time to choose that ones that will allow you to continue respecting yourself and staying away from people and behaviors that injure your self-esteem and confidence.

2. Practice Saying No: A lot of people who have been emotionally/psychologically abuse have difficulty saying no. Due to their codependent traits, they enjoy pleasing people. You may see saying now as being rude, as opposed to being assertive. You are allowed to have needs, and you are not being selfish by being honest about what makes you comfortable and uncomfortable. Practice saying no thank you without explanation, and people will learn to respect your boundaries. Constantly trying to please your abusive partner puts yourself second, on every occasion. It is time now to put yourself first.

3. Look after your own needs: This connects with the previously stated notion. Self-care is very important in all relationships. You have spent most of your life making sure other people are pleased are happy. Now comes the time when it is your turn to prioritize yourself. This can include activities that nurture your soul, your body, your heart, your mind. Learning to engage again with others who genuinely care about you and participate in hobbies

that you love will help you learn that what you want is important too.

4. Learn that you are not responsible for other people's emotions: Being a codependent means that you have spent most of your life taking responsibility for the actions and emotions of other people; i.e., your abuser. You have believed that if something negative happens to them, or if they believe something negative about themselves, that it is your responsibility to fix it. If your partner has an addiction as well as being abusive, you feel extra responsibility for them. But now since you have disengaged, you realize that this is not the truth. If you do not have boundaries, then people will use you as somewhere they can dump their emotional baggage. This is done without thought or consideration for what you can handle. It is normal to share emotions and reactions with people we care about, but it is unhealthy to burden them needlessly with emotions that are not theirs to handle. This can be connected to learning to say no; if someone is bothered by you saying no to an outing, this is not your responsibility. You are learning to make yourself a priority, and your emotions in relation to this matter.

5. Follow through on these boundaries: This will probably one of the hardest positions you will ever find yourself in, but it through the hardest risk that you will earn the most satisfying reward. If you continue practicing setting boundaries, and actually following through on them, you will start respecting yourself, which will be continuing a cycle of self-love rather than abuse.

Chapter 6: CBT Techniques, Problem Solving, Goal Setting and Meditation

This chapter is going to focus on additional skills that can aid you in your ongoing behavior of identifying narcissistic and abusive behavior. It introduces several techniques that are used in cognitive behavioral therapy, a form of psychotherapy that addresses the intermingling of emotions, thoughts, and behaviors. These techniques can help you in the short term while you are miming a plan to depart from your narcissistic abuser, and aid you in a long term manner of self-help. It is recommended that you go through this section with a therapist, who is more qualified to guide you through the process.

In the last section, a few breathing and meditation exercises will be introduced, adding a relaxation element to your prioritizing of self-care.

A Brief History

Cognitive Behavioral Therapy is a form of therapy that focuses on altering unhelpful thoughts and links them and their connection with unhelpful behaviors. Through practical exercises and daily practices, the therapy examines values and beliefs that provide the fodder for unconscious automatic thoughts and their associated behavioral patterns.

There is a long, rich history associated with this form of therapy and how it came to become one of the most recommended and practiced forms of treatment throughout psychiatry and psychotherapeutic institutions. Its history can be linked to three specific waves of thoughts and influences that eventually blended into a single practice; with roots in philosophy, behavioral therapy, and cognitive therapy.

The concept of identifying false beliefs and thoughts can be connected back to initial philosophico traditions such as Stoicism. These type of philosophers believe that logic could be applied to identify the false beliefs that often lead to destructive emotions. Albert Ellis is a key influencing due to his creation of Rational emotive behavior therapy, where he noted many philosophical influences of his own. This form of therapy was one of the first to use empirical evidence sought out by the sufferer to help them understand their surroundings in a more rational way. John Stuart Mill was a British philosopher who also pushed the notion of logic and how it can be connected to the expression and sensation of human emotions.

In the early 20 centuries, behavior therapy became all the rage, the kind of internal reflection that acts outside Freud's psychoanalysis. Work that sat as groundbreaking on the forefront of behaviorism was John B. Watson's discovering of conditioning in 1920. His famously produced study of 'Little Albert' showed how human emotions can become conditioned to certain circumstances. Within his experiment, a young boy named Albert was presented with a white rat, with the associated sound of a loud bell ringing. This elicited fear in the boy. Eventually they stopped ringing the bell, but the boy continued to express fear at the sight of the rat, and any other similarly sized animal later presented to him. Behaviorally cantered therapies appeared as early as 1924, with many practitioner attempting to investigate the root and explanation of childhood fears.

Behavioral therapies and research studies rose up in popularity in the United States, the United Kingdom and South Africa during the 1950s and 1960s. These researchers were influenced by the work of John B. Watson and Ian Pavlov (who discovered classical conditioning; the dog and its association with food to the sound of a bell). Joseph Wolfe of Britain discovered the practice of systematic desensitization, the process in which an anxiety provoking stimulus is presented to a client with a phobia or neurotic disorder until the height of the anxiety lowers and eventually evaporates. Today, within CBT practices, is more commonly referred to as exposure therapy (which will be practiced and discussed within this book).

BF Skinner developed a theory on operant conditioning, the belief that learning proceeds function either through reinforcement or punishment. This belief put very little emphasis on cognition and its association with behavior. In contrast to this theory, Julian Rotter made significant progress on the concept of social learning theory, which states that learning is a both a cognitive process and behavioral process that takes place during observation of other behaviors. They believed that this form of learning can thrive without the presence of reinforcement or punishment.

All of these theories were considered to be what became known as the 'first wave' of CNT. The 'second wave' arose when Alfred Adler began address the relevance of cognition in psychotherapy. His notion of 'basic mistakes' brought the concept of cognition in relation to behavior further into the light of psychotherapy. Around the same time period, Aaron Beck was working as a psychoanalyst and using free association as a method of therapy with his patients (free association is the practice of allowing the patient to speak without intrusion or interruption). During these sessions he noticed that thoughts were not as unconscious as the father of psychoanalysis may have believed, Sigmund Freud. He began to notice too how certain thoughts may act as the trigger for negative emotional states. He began developing cognitive therapy, and started calling these triggering thoughts 'automatic thoughts'. The association between the thoughts and experienced emotions is further explored later on in this book.

There is where Beck started the second wave of CBT.

The third and final wave of CBT sawed the margining of both cognitive and behavioral theories. Early behavioral approaches were successful in treating neurotic disorders (better known now as anxiety disorders), but had very small success in treating those who suffering from depression. Initially, the two-forms of therapy were pitted against one another, but it was the successful treatment of those with panic disorder by David M Clark of the UK that began the merging and understanding that both could work hand-in-hand. Over time, several subtypes of CBT therapies began emerging, such as rational emotive therapy, cognitive therapy, acceptance and commitment therapy, dialectical behavior therapy, reality/choice theory, cognitive processing therapy, and multimodal therapy All of these apply the blending of theories and practices of both behavioral and cognitive treatments.

Goal Setting and Problem-Solving: Depression

One of the main symptoms for those who suffer from debilitating forms of depression is the lack of motivation. If you have suffered from depression or a mood disorder for a long time, it can become easier to feel more and more like you have not achieved much in your life, because your depression is preventing you from doing so. Goal setting and problem solving techniques will each you how to make daily and weekly goals, as well as promoting healthy manners in which you can problem solve without feeling too exasperated.

Setting Goals To Combat Depression

When we feel depressed we can lose sight on our responsibilities, goals, and plans for the future. It is easy to slip into depression, but the further we slip the less focused we are on what gives us purpose and hope for the future. Setting goals helps to combat depression. It helps us stay motivated on our hopes, dreams, and all that life has to offer.

Directions: Complete the questions below to identify your goals for your future.

SHORT-TERM GOALS

What are your goals to complete for this week?

_____

_____

What do you need to achieve these goals?

_____

_____

What are your goals to complete for the next year?

_____

_____

What do you need to meet to complete these goals?

_____

_____

LONG-TERM GOALS

What are your goals to complete for the next 5 years?

_____

_____

What do you need to reach your long-term goals?

_____

_____

LIFE GOALS

Describe what you want your life to be like. What is missing in your life?

_____

_____

What needs to change or improve to be able to live the lifestyle you have described?

_____

_____

Several worksheets will be suggested in this chapter to help you focus on building a happier future. Depression, along with several other mental health disorders, make it difficult to focus on the present moment. One of the ways that can help a depressed person feel grounded is to have their goals laid out in front of them so they can reference them on a daily basis.

This sheet will ask you to outline your goals in three separate distinctions of time: short-term goals, long-term goals, and life goals. It will then be asked what it is that you need in order to achieve these goals. Short-term goals can be anything, from mowing the lawn, to getting up and out of bed by a certain time. Yearly goals can be job applying, or attaining a new job. Long-term and life-goals may seem more intimidating, but when you divide up your life into smaller pieces, longer term goals do not appear as frightening. If you are unable to identify goals that go beyond the short-term, begin by writing weekly goals for a month. Then, try to go back to this worksheet every month, and try to identify later life goals and how you can achieve them for yourself. They do not need to be anything as glamorous as buying a new house or travelling the world. They can be as simple as going on a few dates, reaching out to friends, or learning a new skill.

This next worksheet will focus on how your past is a part of your present, and how you can utilize the present to create a more positive future. It is normal for a person to become stuck in one format of time, whether it be the past or the future, in a negative, depressed or anxious way. This worksheet will help you recognize why your moods were the way that they were in past, and how you can learn to change your behavior to make them different for the present and future. It can also give you a visual understanding of yourself, and cultivate sensations of acceptance and relief, rater

Looking Back, Looking Forward

Being aware of how your past created your present will help you understand how to move into your future.

Directions: Complete the sentences in the table below. Then, list 3 goals to work toward to create a happy and successful future for yourself.

Looking Back	Looking Forward
I was...	I am...
I needed...	I need...
I didn't have...	I have...
I thought...	I know...

Goal 1

Goal 2

Goal 3

than shame and guilt.

It is divided up into three sections: looking back, looking forward, and goal planning. Be as honest with yourself as you can, but also try to begin giving yourself permission to feel compassion and forgiveness. This will prepare you for the later chapter the focus on mindfulness mediation, and relaxed breathing techniques.

After the first two columns are completed, write out three attainable goals. These goals need to be realistic and time-sensitive, more so toward the nearer future than the farthest future. For example, try not to write a goal about winning the lottery.

Learning New Problem Solving Skills

If you suffer from depression, anxiety, or anger issues, it is more than likely that you have trouble solving problems in life. These problems can either relate directly to your mental health, or to other issues that surround it, such as relationship problems, financial problems, or dealing with medical issues. In this section, the most effective forms of problem solving specifically tailored for those who have extra difficulty will be listed, as well as practical steps in how to apply them.

depression.org.nz identifies four steps needed in order to solve a particular problem in a structured format. They have titled it [31]*Structure Problem Solving:*

Step 1: **Identifying Your Problems**: Make a list of the problems you are currently facing. List as many or as little as you would like. Begin by not going into too much detail. Some suggested words that may help you summarize the problem are: relationship with family or spouse, loss or death or someone close, isolation/loneliness, unemployment, harassment or abuse, financial issues, legal issues, substance use issues, physical or mental health issues, low self-esteem or confidence.

1._____

2._____

3._____

4._____

5._____

6._____

---

[31] https://depression.org.nz/assets/Uploads/853bcd2714/structured-problem-solving-workbook.pdf

7._____

8._____

9._____

10. _____

Next, still on this same step, choose a problem that you would like to work on from your list. Once you have chosen one, ask yourself these questions to help you define the problem more clearly:

1. Why is this a problem? What effect does it have on my life?
2. What is the problem?
3. When does this problem occur?
4. Where does the problem occur?
5. Who is involved in this problem?

Once you have answered these questions, try to write out a single sentence that summarizes the problem. Start your statement with the word "I", and include an action word within it. If you do not have control over the problem, then it is going to be difficult to resolve it. Try to choose problems from your list that you have some level of control over.

Step 2: Generating Solutions: Use this section to write down potential solutions for the problem you have just selected. Don't worry for now about whether or not this problem seems realistic or practical. Try not to think too much about it. No matter what ideas come to mind, write them down.

After you have finished writing down all of your potential solutions, take some time to evaluate your list. Eliminate those that are too hard or involve solutions that are not realistic, or involves elements that you are not in control of. Look out for duplicates of solutions.

Choose the best looking ideas that you feel is most practical and likely for you to commit to.

Now it is time for you to evaluate your idea, by weighing out the advantages, disadvantages and neutral components of implementing this solution. Need be, to help you write these out, ask yourself the following questions:

1. How will this solution affect my own well-being? (This means how it will affect you physically, emotionally, and psychologically).
2. How much effort and time is needed?
3. Are there any financial risks involved?
4. Does it fit in with my other daily routines and goals?

5. How will it affect those around me?

6. Is this a feasible solution?

Advantages:

_____

_____

Disadvantages:

_____

_____

Neutral
thoughts:_____

_____

If your idea for a solution has more advantages or neutral thoughts than disadvantages, write out a final statement of this solution. If it does not, go back to your list and solutions and try to find one that has more potential to it.

Step 3: Making an Action Plan: This section will clearly have defined the steps that you need to take in order to make your proposed solution work in the real world. The clearer that you write out an action plan, the more likely that it is going to succeed. This will make it easier to attack the problem head on, and to have something to refer back to when you begin to have trouble.

My   Problem   is:

_____

_____

My   Solution   is:

_____

_____

My plan to do this is:

1. _____

_____

2. _____

_____

3. _____

_____

4. _____

_____

5. _____

_____

6. _____

_____

7. _____

_____

146

8. _____

_____

Write out as many steps as you feel may be necessary in order to complete solving your problem.

Step 4: Review your Progress: Reviewing your progress is an important part of becoming an expert in applying Structured Problem Solving. With every step laid out clearly and concise, you develop a more natural skill of assessing and revolving problems. You will learn as much from your mistakes as you will from your successes. Ask yourself, when reviewing your progress:

1. What   worked well?_____

_____

2. What   didn't   work   as planned?_____

_____

3. What   would   I   change   about   my   plan?

_____

Once you have made your way through this entire section, give yourself a pat on the back! You have taken a big step toward proactively solving issues in your life.

If you feel like you have successfully solved the problem, try to go through the list and apply these steps toward each problem. Even if you have to go through this problems solving section a few times with one problem, try not to be too hard on yourself. There is a reason that they are called problems in the first place

Assertiveness Training for Anger Management

Assertiveness training is another technique applied within CBT treatment. It is specifically used for those who suffer from anger issues. This is because those with issues expressing their anger I have difficultly with communication. Anger is a form of communication, and is a healthy emotion to experience. Letting anger come out through name-calling, blaming, and negative passive-aggressive comments, is not healthy, and can easily effect relationships and your own experience of personal happiness.

If you are having issues expressing your anger, then you may be lacking the skills to be assertive in conversations.

This is a big difference between being aggressive and controlling, then to be confident in validating your needs and desires.

Therefore, there is a difference between expressing anger aggressively and assertively. Expressing your anger assertively means that you are able to express how you feel while being in control of the feelings you are experiencing. Learning to express yourself assertively means separately how you feel with how you express yourself.

If you are having difficultly identifying the differences between being assertive and being aggressive, try to read over this basic summaries:

—-Assertiveness is based on balance: It requires being straightforward about your wants and needs, while still considering these wants and needs of others. You are still applying empathy while firmly getting how you feel across to another person.

—-Aggressive behavior is based on winning: You focus solely on what is in your best interest without thinking about the needs and desires of others. The power you are applying while being aggressive is strictly selfish. You will come across as being a bully or pushy.

[32]*Mind Tools* identifies seven suggested steps that you can follow if you want to develop your assertiveness skills. Applying these will help you to feel more balanced:

1. Value Yourself and Your Rights: Before you try to become more assertive, you should gain a better understanding of yourself. You should also try to develop a strong belief in your natural value of self, as well as your value within a team. Confidence is important when trying to be more assertive, but try not to allow it turn into a sense of self-importance. Your needs, desires, and rights are just as importance as everyone else's.

2. Voice Your Needs and Wants Confidently: If you want to perform at your best level and feel happy in life, you need to make sure your needs and wants are met. Try to identify the things that you want and need now. Set goals (as mentioned in the previous section) so you can look forward to achieving them. Once you have done this, it will be easier to express to those what it is exactly that you need or want. Remember to ask politely, stick to your point, and not to ask others to sacrifice their own needs for yours.

3. Acknowledge That You Can't Control Other People's Behaviors: This is an important fact for those with anger issues to realize. Oftentimes, we become angry with people

[32] https://www.mindtools.com/pages/article/Assertiveness.htm

when they do things that do not line up with what we want. But we cannot control what other people do, and it is important to keep remind yourself of that fact. You can only focus on your own behavior. As long as you are respecting the needs of others, then you have the right to say what you want.

4. Learn to Express Yourself in a Positive Way: Falling into negative behaviors and expressions of anger is very easy. Try to focus on expressing what you need positively, even if you are feeling angry. This will help you not fall into the bad habit of name-calling, accusing, etc.

5. Be Open to Criticism and Compliments: Try to develop the skill of accepting both positive and negative feedback. Sometimes, when you receive negative feedback, it is easy to start feeling defensive, and even hurt. If you do not agree with the feedback you are receiving, then you need to prepare yourself to say so. Again, this is meant to be expressed assertively, without anger or aggressiveness.

6. Learn to Say No: People who suffer with issues when being assertive often have difficultly saying no. Saying no is important when considering your own wants and needs, as well as contracting boundaries that are healthy and necessary. You are not able to please everyone, nor are you and endless source of energy. Saying no to people in your relationships, job settings, and friends shows that you know what you want and need, and respect yourself enough to follow through on them.

7. Using Assertive Communication Techniques: There are a number of ways that you can apply certain assertive skills through the practice of some of these techniques:

—-Use "I" Statements: Using the word "I" conveys the basic assertion that you want to get your point across firmly. It also avoids blaming and the escalation of pointless arguments.

—-Empathy: It is hard when you are angry to try to see the issues from another person's point of view. But if you practice empathy on a consistent basis, the level in which your anger reaches will begin to lower each time you feel you are going to overreact. If you see a situation from another person's point of view, it is easier to understand the reasoning behind their behavior. You still don't have to agree with the person, but it will help your anger feel more constructive rather than destructive.

—-Escalation: Trying to be assertive with another person isn't always going to work the first time you apply it. Maine that person also has issues with anger, and expressing themselves/Some problems also require more time and patience in order to be resolved, such as problems in the workplace. If you feel you need to escalate your assertiveness, continue along the path of being polite and respectful, but firm.

—-Ask for more Time: If you can feel your anger rising and identify that you are having trouble controlling it, feel enough confidence to ask for some time so your anger can dissipate, and you can choose a reaction that is more rational.

—-Change Your Verbs: Try integrated verbs into your vocabulary that clearly and firmly state what it is your asking for, or what it is that you need. When you do this, there will be more room for misinterpretation. Begin using words like "will" instead of "could/should", and "want" instead of "need", "choose to" instead of "have to".

—-Don't be afraid to sound like a Broken Record: Keep reiterating yourself if a person is not taking what you are saying seriously. Continue you using the strong and firm message until the person will realize that you are drawing a line and are meaning what you're saying. This is best to practice at work if you are overwhelmed with tasks, and someone tries to throw more onto, using guilt as a weapon. No matter what they say, stick with your assertive statement that lets them know you cannot take on anymore work. Your needs are important.

—-Try Scripting: Scripting is a technique that allows you to practice making assertive statements before you may need to state them. It will help you prepare what you are going to say, and give you enough confidence to stick to it:

1. The Event: Tell the other person exactly how you see the issue.
2. Your Feelings: Describe how you feel about the situation and express them as clearly as possible.
3. Your needs: Tell the person exactly what it is that you need from them so they do not have to guess.

4. The Consequences: Describe the positive effect that your request will have for the other person if you need are actually met.

Write down the observe steps in your notebook if this is an occurrence you want to practice being assertive about. Applying assertiveness instead of being angry will in the long run help you in your relationships, your work life, and will help you live a more enjoyable and fulfilling life.

Relaxed Breath Techniques

Relaxation techniques are meant to work best in conjunction with exposure therapy as well as cognitive restructuring. The point of breathing exercises and relaxation techniques is not to replace the sensation of anxiety, depression or anger, or to run from it, but to embrace it, and help you learn the difference between thoughts and physical sensations. These techniques will help you become more aware of how your body reacts to certain thoughts and moods. Please take note of when you feel you may be using one of those techniques in order to flee from the unpleasant feeling. This is not the point of them, and will only injure your progress in the long run.

Breathing Exercises: Slow Diaphragmatic Breathing

This technique sends a direct signal to the brain to let it know that it is safe. This practice is usually recommended to be done alone, either before your start your day or after it. You can apply it while you are in a situation that makes you anxious, or are coping with a memory or triggered depressive thoughts. But remember, you are not doing this to rid yourself of the anxiety. If you are doing it in the moment, remember that it is meant to have the emotion felt, and to remind you that you are safe.

5. From a comfortable chair with your feet on the floor, or find a place to lie down.

6. Place your hands onto your belly and allow them to rest gently.

7. Start by observing your breath. Try not to judge the pace in which your belly is rising and falling.

8. Begin filling up your belly with an inhale slow, so it starts to feel like a little beach ball or globe. Imagine a balloon being filled up. Do not do this roughly or too fast. Focus on breathing into your stomach, and not allowing your shoulders to lift as you inhale.

9. Breathe out slowly to the count of five. Try to do this as slowly as possible.

10. After the exhale, hold for about 2-3 seconds before you inhale into your belly again.

11. Breathe in and out this way and observe how your breath has slowed down.

12. Practice this for around 10 minutes.

This practice will work better if you try to do this twice a day at the beginning of your treatment. Try to do it at the same point of the day, every day. This is usually a good start for those who suffer from anxiety or anger issues.

Progressive Muscle Relaxation

Many people with anxiety, depression and anger issues suffer from muscle tension. For the person with anxiety, it is because when they experience the emotion of that anxiety in their body, their muscle tense up, as a reaction toward a perceived threat (to either participate in fight or flight). People with repressed anger issues suffer from the same problem. Those with depression are know to possess extra tense muscles because of the constant ruminating that causes immense stress within their bodies.

For whatever reason it may be, this technique attempts to employ the opposite. It is the absence of tension in the body's muscles. The aim of it is to gradually learn to release tension in the muscles through daily exercise. This shows your body during moments of anxiety and/or anger that you are safe, and reduces the likelihood of a flight or fight response. The practice has you systematically tensing and relaxing certain muscle groups of the body. If you try it out for a moment and tense your bicep now, for about 5-7 seconds, then allow it to relax, you feel the instant difference in the lack of tension.

If you have a history of other medical problems, please consult with your local physician about using this relaxation exercise:

13. You will be stating at your feet and working your way up to your face. Make yourself comfortable with loose clothing, and either sit upright on a chair or lie down.
14. Take a few minutes to breathe in and out slowly, with deep breaths.
15. When you feel ready, shift your attention to your right foot. Observe it without judgment.
16. Slowly, begin tensing the muscles in your right foot, squeezing as tightly as you are physically able to. Hold for a count to 10.
17. Slowly relax your foot. Focus on the tension slowly leaking out as your foot gets loose and limp.
18. Stay in this moment for a few seconds, breathing slowly and deeply.
19. Shift your attention to your left food.
20. Follow these steps for each section of your body.

If you are unsure about which muscles you should tense at the same or separate moment, try following this miniature guideline:

—-Right foot, left foot.

—-Right calf, left calf.

—-Right thigh, left thigh.

—-Buttocks and hips.

—-Stomach.

—-Chest.

—-Back.

—-Right arm and hand, left arm and hand.

—-Shoulders and neck.

—-Face.

It may take some time for you to adjust to tensing the right body muscles, but do not be too hard on yourself. You are slowly teaching your body to calm down.

Body Scan Meditation

This meditation is a relaxed breath technique that blends together concepts of progressive muscle relaxation and deep breathing. It focuses your attention on various parts of your body as well, but instead of tensing and relaxing them, you will simply focus on the way each part of your body feels, and avoid labelling the sensations as something positive or negative.

21. Lie on your back with your legs uncrossed, arms relaxed at your sides. You can have your eyes either open or closed, but if they are open, try not to focus on anything in particular. Focus on your breathing for about two minutes so you can become relaxed.

22. Begin by focusing on the toes of your right foot. Notice any sensations that might be lurking there, whether it be tingling, an itch, or nothing at all. Focus on it while imagining each deep breath flowing through your toes. Stay on this area for about 1-2 minutes.

23. Move onto the sole of your foot. Then move onto the right foot and repeat.

24. Move to your calf, knee, thigh, hip on your right side. Then the left side.

25. Once you have observed both sides, practice this observation on your torso, lower back and abdomen, the upper back and chest, and shoulders. Finally, end on your neck, your face, and the top of your head.

26. Once you have focused on each part of your body for around 1-2 minutes each, relax for a while in silence and stillness, noticing how your body is feeling.

27. Slowly open your eyes.

This form of mediation teaches you that whatever you may be feeling your body is fine as it is, and does not require a label that falls under the category of either bad or good. This is an attempt to retrain your mind and no longer find negative associations between certain bodily sensations and the anticipation of oncoming doom.

Mindfulness: The Benefits

Mindfulness is a practice that has grown in popularity and is often integrated into various forms of therapeutic treatment. Mindfulness is defined as a practice that longs to keep you in the present moment without the desire to flee from whatever feeling, bodily sensation, or behavioral issue may be plaguing you. Many mental health issues thrive on either dwelling on the past, or obsessing over the future. Mindfulness practices help you learn to observe your thoughts without judgment or criticismi, and to teach you how to begin cultivating compassion toward yourself and your experiences.

Mindfulness Meditation

Mindfulness meditation is not just meant for monks. Many people misunderstand what the point of mindful mediation is. An image of someone hovering over the clouds on a mountaintop is a commonly associated misconception. Mindfulness meditation is not practice meant for an elect few. It is meant to be practice by anyone and everyone, no matter what age or point they are in their lives. No matter how busy, stressed, anxious, angry, or unhappy you may be, mindfulness meditation will act as another tool to integrate into your self-care toolbox. It has been successful to help people in the past reduce stress, anxiety, depression, and anger issues.

Depending on what kind of mindfulness meditation you are participating in, the practice will help you by focusing your attention either on a single repetitive action, such as breathing, or encourage you to observe a specific portion of your mind. Some practices ask you to observe your thoughts without judgment or criticism, so you can learn that thoughts are just as they are; not you at all. It can also be applied to several activities that involve movement, such as walking, eating, or exercising.

Here is a simple exercise of mindful meditation that you can begin practicing now:

28. Find a quiet, comfortable space where you know you will not be interrupted or distracted.
29. Sit on a chair that is straight-backed, or sit crossed-legged on the floor.

30. Choose a point of focus; most people like to focus on their breathing at first. It can be the sensation of air moving in and out of your nostrils, your belly rising and falling, or a candle flame or meaningful word you repeated through the practice.
31. Distracting thoughts do not mean you are 'doing it wrong'. Your mind is like a monkey, and is meant to be playing around. If you find yourself becoming distracted, do not be angry. The point is to simply bring your attention back to the selected focus of attention, not matter how many times your mind tries to run off.

Visualization

This is a guided imagery practice and a variation on tradition mediation that involves the imagining of a scene that helps you to feel calm. Each person will have a different scene that makes them feel calm; it can be a beach, a childhood home, or even just your bed at home. You can do visualization either on your own or with a therapist. Aids such as soothing music help some people visualize better, along with sounds that co-inside with your particular location.

Here is an easy visualization exercise that can help you get started:

32. Close your eyes. Be sure to do this in a place where you are not distracted or unsafe.
33. Find music, sounds, or rhythmic tones that will help your experience feel more authentic. These can be found through YouTube, or through a simple google search.
34. Picture your peaceful place as vividly as you can; make note of the sounds, sights, smells, feels, and tastes.
35. Some people lose track of where they are during a visualization, have heavy limbs, or begin yawning. If this happens to you, don't worry, it is a very common reaction.

If you are unsure as to which practice may benefit you most, try utilizing one day for the next week. You will then begin to notice which ones you feel more comfortable practicing or receive the most benefits from.

Remember, that relaxed breathing techniques and visualization are not practices that are meant to be cure-alls for your mental health issues. They are one part of many building blocks that are going to help you understand your own unique mental health experience. So continue keeping up the review of cognitive distortions and exposure therapy.

Conclusion

"You can be certain that the winner in the end will be you, with your mind and soul Intact. You have pinpointed the heart of the matter. You can love, will always be able to love. He can't, and never will. He Is an emotional cripple who cannot even love himself. You will move forward in life, but he will remain, always. In the shadow-lands of his disorder."

Abuse in summary, is a difficult cycle to break. It is never as simple as just leaving the person who continuously reduces your self-worth, self-esteem, and confidence. If an individual respected themselves and had high self-esteem, they would never fall into the trap of a narcissistic abuser. The abuser is smart and tactical about the ways in which they choose to treat their victim. They are also specific about who they choose to behave this way toward; they are drawn toward people who feel fulfillment about helping a person feel good about themselves, aka, a codependent person. Since the codependent is drawn to the narcissistic, this relationship clicks, and often thrives for a fair amount of time.

As this book has described, out of all of the forms of abuse, emotional/psychological is the most difficult to identify. This is the case when the victim is an adult, a child, or an elderly person. Unlike physical or sexual abuse, results cannot be viewed visually by a third party. It is dependent upon what stage of change a person is in in a domestic relationship as to whether or not they can admit that abuse is occurring. This is the most important step in the healing process for victims of abuse. Admitting that their interaction between them and their partner is abuse makes them realize that there exists a world where they are treated better, and seeking out this world is a possible reality.

Guilt, shame, name-calling, humiliation, gaslighting, and threats are some of the ways that narcissistic personalities emotionally/psychologically abuse their victims. It is through the cycle of abuse that confuses the victims, as they go through the roundabout behaviors of calm, the build-up, the incident phase, and then the reconciliation. There are times when they are kind, charming, seemingly giving and caring. This is what will keep someone with another as their partner, because the existence of anything positive justifies how 'good' the person is, which allows them to excuse the negative behavior when it occurs.

Change is possible, and escape does happen. People of all ages, genders, cultural backgrounds and orientation are capable of moving on and living lives that satisfy them, without the constant negative presence of an abuser. You too can begin a new life and learn that you are loveable, and can be cherished by other people in your life by simply being who you are, rather then merely existing to satisfy the needs of others.

SIMONDYER MILLER

Printed in Great
Britain
by Amazon

31418517R00099